# SOCIAL CLASS IN EUROPE

# SOCIAL CLASS
# IN EUROPE

## NEW INEQUALITIES IN THE OLD WORLD

CÉDRIC HUGRÉE, ETIENNE PENISSAT
AND ALEXIS SPIRE

TRANSLATED BY RACHEL GOMME
WITH EUNICE SANYA PELINI

VERSO
London • New York

First published in English by Verso 2020
First published as *Les Classes sociales en Europe. Tableau
des nouvelles inégalités sur le vieux continent*
© Editions Agone 2017
Translation © Rachel Gomme with Eunice Sanya Pelini 2020

1 3 5 7 9 10 8 6 4 2

**Verso**
UK: 6 Meard Street, London W1F 0EG
US: 20 Jay Street, Suite 1010, Brooklyn, NY 11201
versobooks.com

Verso is the imprint of New Left Books

ISBN-13: 978-1-78873-628-2
ISBN-13: 978-1-78873-627-5 (LIBRARY)
ISBN-13: 978-1-78873-630-5 (UK EBK)
ISBN-13: 978-1-78873-629-9 (US EBK)

**British Library Cataloguing in Publication Data**
A catalogue record for this book is available from the British Library

**Library of Congress Cataloging-in-Publication Data**
Library of Congress Control Number:
2020932681

Typeset in Minion by Hewer Text (UK) Ltd, Edinburgh
Printed and bound by CPI Group (UK) Ltd, Croydon CR0 4YY

# Contents

# Maps

# Graphs

# Tables

# Abbreviations

AT: Austria
BE: Belgium
BG: Bulgaria
CY: Cyprus
CZ: Czech Republic
DE: Germany
DK: Denmark
EE: Estonia
ES: Spain
FI: Finland
FR: France
GR: Greece
HU: Hungary
IE: Ireland
IT: Italy
LT: Lithuania
LU: Luxembourg
LV: Latvia
NL: Netherlands
PL: Poland
PT: Portugal
RO: Romania
SE: Sweden
SK: Slovakia
SL: Slovenia
UK: United Kingdom

EC: European Community
ECB: European Central Bank
EU: European Union
GDP: Gross Domestic Product
IMF: International Monetary Fund
OECD: Organisation for Economic Co-operation and
  Development

AES: Adult Education Survey
EWCS: European Working Conditions Survey
LFS: Labour Force Survey

EU-SILC: European Union Statistics on Income and Living
  Conditions

# Acknowledgements

A first version of this book was published in French, entitled *Les classes sociales en Europe* (Paris: Agone, 2017). The initial idea came from Cécile Brousse, whose work inspired us a lot. Access to European surveys was first made possible by our participation in the ESEG research group at the Institut national de la SEE. Our three laboratories, CERAPS, IRIS and CRESPPA-CSU, provided us with logistical and financial support for the publication. Our bibliographical research benefited from the suggestions of several colleagues who helped us to better understand social class in different countries: Virgilio Borges Pereira, Bruno Monteiro, Angeliki Drongiti, Jani Erola, Mihaela Hainagiu, Michał Kozłowski, Clemence Ledoux, Thomas Maloutas, Enrique Martin Criado, Pablo Lopez Calle, Harri Melin, Mikael Palme, Andreas Melldahl, Marie Plessz, Spyros Sakellaropoulos and Yiorgos Vassalos. Thanks to these correspondents, we were able to feed our demonstration of qualitative research conducted in different European countries.

Thomas Amossé, Philippe Askenazy, Audrey Mariette, Tristan Poullaouec and Delphine Serre reviewed all or part of the manuscript and offered us valuable suggestions. The remaining imperfections are obviously our sole responsibility.

The entire text was translated by Rachel Gomme, with the exception of chapters 2 and 3, which were translated by Eunice Sanya Pelini.

# Introduction

The European Union has become the subject of intense conflict, as evinced by the 'no' votes in the French and Dutch referendums on the constitutional treaty in 2005, the Greek debt crisis of 2010, and the vote for Brexit in June 2016. In every country in Europe, an enduring political split has opened up between supporters and opponents of the European project.[1] Supporters take the view that this project represents the best way of ensuring economic progress and business competitiveness through the increase in trade; for opponents, it encourages social dumping and brings down standards of living for the majority. The tensions caused by relocations and competition between workers lead certain groups to demand protection for their national space. In response to these anxieties, journalists and politicians usually adopt a simplistic frame of reference that pits *insiders* against *outsiders*, globalisation's winners against its losers, with the stereotype of the Polish plumber competing with the French, German or British worker. Although the social question lies at the heart of this political conflict, very few recorded data are available on social inequalities between European workers. In political discussions on the subject, the EU bureaucracy is rigidly tied to austerity,[2] and no mention is ever made of class distinction as a key tool of comprehension. It is time to ask what the famous Polish plumber has in common with a Romanian senior manager

---

1    Hans-Jörg Trenz, Carlo Ruzza and Virginie Guiraudon (eds.), *Europe's Prolonged Crisis: The Making or the Unmaking of a Political Union*, Basingstoke: Palgrave Macmillan, 2016.
2    Yanis Varoufakis, *Adults in the Room: My Battle with Europe's Deep Establishment*, London: The Bodley Head, 2017.

or a Spanish manual worker, and what sets them apart from one another.

The aim of this book is to present a map of inequalities in Europe that goes beyond the usual comparisons between countries: drawing on statistical data that are very rarely analysed from the point of view of occupations, our aim is to give an account for the first time of the differences between social classes at the European level.[3] The point is not to ignore national specificities: people born in wealthiest countries keep what Milanovic called 'citizenship rent'.[4] Thanks to the World Inequality Database, it is now possible and easy to compare the level of income in one country with other incomes in Europe.[5] Here, we would rather like to show how the national differences are embedded in a convergence of social inequalities that prevail in all European countries. In our view, the issue of inequality cannot be reduced to a simple analysis of levels of income and assets: it also relates to conditions of employment and work, lifestyles, housing conditions, cultural practices and leisure. These various domains of social life can now be measured through statistical studies conducted consistently in all European countries. Our task, then, is to consider the disparities between socio-economic and national groups, as well as gender and generational differences, together as a whole. Our commitment to an analysis in terms of social class is also a political act: more than just describing inequalities, our aim is to investigate the conditions of possibility of a European social movement.

## CONSIDERING EUROPE THROUGH THE LENS OF SOCIAL CLASS

Since the 1980s, while European integration has gathered pace, the representation of society in terms of social class has been consistently

---

3    The use of the plural is due in part to the desire to think together the oppositions between social classes, but also between class-fractions, internal to these social classes.

4    Branko Milanovic, *Global Inequality: A New Approach for the Age of Globalization*, London: Harvard University Press, 2016, 132.

5    See wid.world/simulator.

declining. In the West, the retreat of Marxism resulted in a decline in the use of this concept in public debate, while in the East the desire for a radical break with the vestiges of Stalinism made it a despised term.

On both sides of the continent, the outlines of social classes are less distinct than they were in the past. Changes in European economic structures have played a substantial role in this process. The decline of industry and the growth of the service and retail sectors, the continuing rise in jobs in management and intermediate occupations, as well as mass unemployment, have substantially blurred the boundaries between social classes, while marginalising the industrial proletariat which used to comprise the hard core of the working class. The extension of duration of studies, and the spread of media and digital technology, have also revivified forms of inequality between countries and within different European social groups.

On the political level, the disappearance of the communist states and the weakening of workers' parties and trade unions in Western countries have to some extent delegitimised references to class struggle. More generally, people no longer use class as a way of locating themselves within the social space. Throughout Europe, the sense of belonging to the working class has diminished among manual workers and low-skilled white-collar workers,[6] and been replaced by the feeling of belonging to a vast middle class. Even when social protest regains momentum, as with the anti-austerity movements that arose in response to the 2008 crisis, the activists thus mobilised do not make their arguments in terms of class antagonism, but base their demands on more vague and encompassing oppositions, such as the division between the richest 1 per cent and the remaining 99 per cent, or between 'the oligarchy' and 'the people'. These various developments have revived the idea

---

6   The gender distribution in the employment structure is not equal: women form the majority in some social groups, and men in others. The original French text therefore uses the feminine gender to refer to certain social groups, in particular low-skilled white-collar workers in the retail and service sectors, office workers and domestic cleaners. While English has no equivalent expression, where reference is made to these groups it should be borne in mind that they are overwhelmingly female. Obviously, this does not mean that these groups contain no men, nor conversely that those groups identified as male are exclusively composed of men.

that social class is disappearing.[7] When reference is made to 'twenty-first-century class conflicts', it is either in relation to non-European territories or in predictions of the development of a precariat whose common characteristic is the lack of a stable job and career possibilities.[8]

The notion of class, articulated as the political and symbolic construction of a vision of the social world,[9] is thus far less central today than it was in the past. Nevertheless, class status remains a pertinent tool for reflecting on and describing inequalities and social boundaries on the international level.[10] We are also seeing renewed interest in using it as a way of reflecting on inequality in European societies.[11] In France, the Yellow vests ("*gilets jaunes*") revolt that broke out in November 2018 put the working classes back at the centre of the public debate: starting as a challenge to increased fuel duty, the protest widened to demands around purchasing power and for the greater use of referendums. Several calls for extension to other countries were made, with unsuccessful attempts in both Wallonia (Belgium) and Poland. The confinement of the Yellow vests within French borders illustrates the difficulty faced by social movements in raising the issue of inequalities on a European scale.

Is it possible to speak of a European working class or a transnational ruling class? Class relations are largely constructed in

7   Jan Pakulski and Malcolm Waters, 'The Reshaping and Dissolution of Social Class in Advanced Society', *Theory and Society* 25: 5, 1996, 667–91; Geoffrey Evans (ed.), *The End of Class Politics: Class Voting in Comparative Context*, Oxford: Oxford University Press, 1999; Terry N. Clark and Seymour M. Lipset (eds.), *The Breakdown of Class Politics: A Debate on Post-industrial Stratification*, Washington, DC: Woodrow Wilson Center Press and Johns Hopkins University Press, 2001.

8   For these two approaches, see respectively Göran Therborn, 'Class in the 21st Century', *New Left Review* 78: 5, 2012, 5–29; and Guy Standing, *The Precariat: The New Dangerous Class*, London: Bloomsbury Academic, 2011.

9   Pierre Bourdieu, 'The Social Space and the Genesis of Groups', *Theory and Society* 14: 6, 1985, 723–44.

10   Anne-Catherine Wagner, *Les classes sociales dans la mondialisation*, Paris: La Découverte, 2007.

11   Fiona Devine, Mike Savage, John Scott and Rosemary Crompton, *Rethinking Class: Culture, Identities and Lifestyle*, Basingstoke: Palgrave Macmillan, 2005.

the context of nation states, and in each country the outlines and intensity of these relations are shaped by the specific social and political history of the nation. Conversely, the European Union is not a state: it currently has no sovereign authority, apart from very limited prerogatives in specific areas such as immigration. And, while it has its own bureaucracy, its own staff and its own systems,[12] its social policy is virtually non-existent. Its principal intervention, often with the support of the International Monetary Fund (IMF), has been to demand reforms requiring ever greater flexibility on the part of European workers, particularly since the start of the crisis in 2008.

In fact, until now, there have been few studies of inequality that consider the issue in terms of class at the European level. Yet this is a frame of reference, and even of identification, that is increasingly important for the people of Europe. The existence of institutions that provide resources, of financial regulations, norms, regular electoral processes and recognised symbols (flags, anthem), mark it as a social and political space. Moreover, the European Union represents a huge market, within which the various member states maintain particularly strong economic relations: nearly two-thirds of the trade of EU countries is within the European Union.

On a more fundamental level, most of the contemporary socio-economic changes are occurring at supranational level, from the managerial turn of states to political developments, from the transformation of cities to changes in the education system and the restructuring of industry.[13] The circulation, localisation and

12  Didier Georgakakis and Jay Rowell, *The Field of Eurocracy: Mapping the EU Staff and Professionals*, Basingstoke: Palgrave Macmillan, 2013.

13  For these domains, see, respectively, Patrick Le Galès and Desmond King (eds.), *Reconfiguring European States in Crisis*, Oxford: Oxford University Press, 2017; Adrian Favell and Virginie Guiraudon (eds.), *Sociology of the European Union*, New York: Palgrave Macmillan, 2011; Arnaldo Bagnasco and Patrick Le Galès (eds.), *Cities in Contemporary Europe*, Cambridge: Cambridge University Press, 2000; Tim Butler and Agnes van Zanten, 'School Choice: A European Perspective', *Journal of Education Policy* 22: 1, 2007, 1–5; Michael Faust, Ulrich Voskamp and Volker Wittke (eds.), *European Industrial Restructuring in a Global Economy: Fragmentation and Relocation of Value Chains*, Göttingen: SOFI, 2004.

specialisation of capital contribute to forming and shaping class relations in Europe as a whole: the French executive directors of Danone invest in land belonging to Polish farmers; German senior managers at vehicle manufacturer Audi employ and manage workers in factories in Belgium, Spain and Hungary; Romanian forestry workers come to work in French forests; Polish workers are seconded to subcontracting companies in the shipyards at Saint-Nazaire in France; and so on. Capitalism has become extensively Europeanised, and class relations along with it. National corporations remain important but there is a concentration process in the big economic and financial firms: according to foreign direct investment figures, European multinationals have greatly increased their foreign investment in the last two decades: from 10 per cent to 60 per cent of GDP in Europe.[14] There are more and more firms operating across multiple European countries.

The economic strategies of large European companies thus play a major part in determining the morphology of social classes in different European countries. The acquisition of an MBA or a degree from a prestigious foreign university has now become an essential rite of passage for those aspiring to managerial posts within the economic elites; similarly, more and more company directors play up their professional experience in a multinational as a way of establishing their legitimacy.[15] At the same time, the mobility of workers within the European Union has risen since the union was expanded to include countries from the former East.[16] There are two particularly significant movements of

---

14 Tristan Auvray and Cédric Durand, 'A European Capitalism? Revisiting the Mandel–Poulantzas Debate', in Jean-Numa Ducange and Razmig Keucheyan (eds.), *The End of the Democratic State*, trans. by David Broder, Cham: Palgrave Macmillan, 2019, 145–65.

15 William K. Carroll, *The Making of a Transnational Capitalist Class: Corporate Power in the 21st Century*, London: Zed Books, 2010.

16 For the sake of convenience, we distinguish regularly between several groups of countries: 'countries of the North and West': Austria, Belgium, Denmark, Finland, France, Germany, Ireland, Luxembourg, the Netherlands, Sweden, the UK; 'countries of the South': Cyprus, Greece, Italy, Portugal, Spain; 'countries of Central and Eastern Europe': Bulgaria,

labour: the first from Bulgaria and Romania to Spain and Italy, and the second from the countries of the former East to the United Kingdom, Ireland and Germany. The substantial increase (over 45 per cent) in the number of posted workers in Europe between 2010 and 2014 is one illustration of this: today there are over two million of them in the European Union. In other words, class relations are experienced over the territory of Europe as a whole, not just at national level. Following the 'no' vote in the French and Dutch referendums of 2005, many interpreted the result as the revenge of the working class on the elite, in the context of a conflict that was now being played out on the European stage. The same was true of the Brexit vote in the United Kingdom,[17] even though, in some cases, the contribution of working-class voters to these great electoral jamborees was a refusal to participate.[18] Behind what are often presented as oppositions between national identities lie political conflicts rooted in class divisions.

---

Czech Republic, Estonia, Hungary, Latvia, Lithuania, Poland, Romania, Slovakia and Slovenia. In order not to appear to reduce these last countries to their history as former socialist states, we have systematically avoided using the isolated expressions 'countries of the East' or 'Eastern Europe', with their strong associations with the Cold War period. Nevertheless, we shall on occasion make reference to the 'countries of the former East' when our aim is specifically to emphasise that history. These geographical distinctions refer to groups of countries as they were successively integrated into the European Union, and to some extent overlap with inequalities in the distribution of economic activity, resources, the shape of socio-economic groups and the relative proportion of social class. However, in order not to reify these subgroups, we shall draw more finely detailed distinctions throughout this book.

17   According to a YouGov poll, 37 per cent of skilled manual workers (C2) voted to remain in the EU, compared to 57 per cent of white-collar workers (ABC1).

18   In the European elections of 1999 and 2004, for example, participation was lower among those who felt they belonged to the working class than among those who said they belonged to the middle or upper classes. Sara B. Hobolt, Jae-Jae Spoon and James Tilley, 'A Vote against Europe? Explaining Defection at the 1999 and 2004 European Parliament Elections', *British Journal of Political Science* 39: 1, 2009, 93–115.

The few studies that exist of social class at the European level make little use of empirical data, and in the absence of statistical inquiry, ultimately make excessively abstract cases. One example is American sociologist Neil Fligstein, who, in his provocatively titled book *Euro-Clash*, argues that Europe can be split into three classes. At the top, he places a transnational elite of people who travel widely, speak several languages and identify themselves with the European project, from which they benefit both materially and culturally. In the middle there is a group of mainly middle-class citizens which is more sporadically connected with Europe, through either vacations, leisure (football, for example) or a professional occupation linked to the European economy. At the bottom there is a third, poorer group with a lower level of education, who speak only the language of their own country and do not consume cultural goods imported from other countries.[19]

Although it is only minimally based on the actual social position of individuals, Fligstein's book thus invites us to think about class divisions at the European level. In fact, it is now possible to identify social groups precisely, using the large-scale European statistical surveys. The aim of the present study is to consider skilled manual workers, farmers or executives at the same level of detail over the whole of Europe. To what extent can similarity of social conditions outweigh the individual specificities of countries of residence? And, if national identity remains important, is it nevertheless possible to identify stronger European convergences between, for example, the elites in different countries than between the working and middle classes of any one country?

## TRANSCENDING THE CLICHÉS OF NATIONAL DIFFERENCE

Arguing for an empirical sociology of social class in Europe means taking the opposite view from that disseminated by the European

---

19   Neil Fligstein, *Euro-Clash: The EU, European Identity, and the Future of Europe*, Oxford: Oxford University Press, 2008.

Commission, which remains anchored to a division along national boundaries. The commission, via Eurostat (the statistical office of the European Union), supervises the publication of data provided by national statistical bodies (rate of growth, percentage of national debt, etc.), and publishes data on the operation of job markets (levels of employment and unemployment) that tend to underscore national differences. For example, per capita income varies widely from one country to another: the highest, that of Luxembourg, is three times that of the lowest, Romania.[20] But the lens through which the European Commission views these matters is often highly restrictive and distorting. It effectively serves to compare countries with one another, in order either to validate the idea that inequalities can only be described at national level, or to set states in competition with one another. Official sources sometimes use other criteria, such as levels of education, but this is usually for the purpose of contrasting the 'good student' countries with the 'poor students' of Europe. Reference to social class, on the other hand, or even to socio-economic groups, is never used as a marker. Who knows how many farmers, skilled manual workers, senior managers or CEOs there are in Europe? While state development in France and the United Kingdom is based on statistical accounting in terms of social groups,[21] this frame of reference is totally absent at European level. The unemployment rate is a good example of this bias, with significant political import: by emphasising differences in unemployment rates between countries, the statistics published by European institutions highlight disparities in economic performance while masking inequality of exposure to unemployment between the working class and the dominant class.

During the crisis in the eurozone in the late 2000s, arguments that were centred on national differences, sometimes embellished

20  In 2018, the gross national income per inhabitant (in terms of purchasing-power parity) was $23,900 in Romania compared to $60,869 in Luxembourg (*Source*: World Bank).

21  Alain Desrosières, *The Politics of Large Numbers: A History of Statistical Reasoning*, Cambridge, MA: Harvard University Press, 2002.

with culturalist stereotypes, became increasingly powerful: on the one hand there were the countries stigmatised by the term PIIGS (Portugal, Ireland, Italy, Greece and Spain) on the ground of their alleged inability to pay their national debt, suspected of being lazy, irresponsible and even corrupt; on the other were Germany and the countries of the North, depicted as disciplined, hard-working and honest. These generalisations, which echo Montesquieu's old theory of climates, whereby the climate influenced the nature of human beings and their societies, have powerfully pervaded discourses and representations. In contrast to this thinking, our approach will seek to identify the European populations and social groups that have been most affected by the opening up of national economies to competition.

When European institutions do take an interest in inequalities between individuals, it is mainly from the point of view of 'human capital', defined as the set of qualifications, aptitudes, skills and experience accumulated by individuals over the course of their life. In a society where education has become universal, access to life-long education is portrayed as the means of giving each person the 'chance' of social mobility or access to employment. This vision is manifested in the European Commission's voluntarist policy of developing the 'human capital' of European citizens. The European Union has set itself the goal of improving levels of education by 2020, with the aim of increasing individuals' employability. The two principal objectives that have been put into figures are increasing the proportion of people who have been awarded a higher education qualification, and reducing the proportion of young people who leave education and training early, an area where there are wide variations between countries. However, universal access to education does not automatically translate into a reduction in social inequality, since working-class children always have great difficulty in converting their qualifications into social positions as advantageous as those of children of the middle and dominant classes.[22] Moreover, this institutional approach tends to reduce

---

22  Yossi Shavit (ed.), *Stratification in Higher Education: A Comparative Study*, Stanford: Stanford University Press, 2007.

inequality to a matter of education alone, while inequalities constructed in the workplace, and in housing, leisure and sociality, remain hidden.

## BEYOND INCOME INEQUALITY

The depth of the 2008 financial and economic crisis put the issue of wealth differences between social groups back on the agenda. Thomas Piketty, in *Capital in the Twenty-First Century*, profoundly reworked an economic analysis which had, until then, been focused on differences in income: his book revealed that possession of assets – that is, capital that over the long term grows more rapidly than the production of added value – lies at the heart of contemporary inequalities.[23] In the context of financial globalisation and weakening systems of social protection, wealth inequality becomes central. But power relations cannot be reduced to the action of a few 'super-rich' people whose income has skyrocketed compared to the rest of the population. They play out at many other levels on the social scale – between the foreman and his subordinate, or between the private-sector manager and her children's babysitter – and they are constructed in all the various areas of social life. Moreover, defining inequality solely in terms of income tends to conceal not only the political power relations between social groups, but also the internal divisions within them.[24] The notion of class allows us to distinguish not only the lack of resources or the dependence of the working class in relation to the middle class and the dominant class, but also an equally determining factor, what Olivier Schwartz calls the 'assignment of low and subordinate status'

---

23    Thomas Piketty, *Capital in the Twenty-First Century*, Cambridge, MA: Harvard University Press, 2014.

24    John H. Goldthorpe and Abigail McKnight, 'The Economic Basis of Social Class. Mobility and Inequality: Frontiers of Research from Sociology and Economics', in Morgan Grusky (ed.), *Mobility and Inequality*, Stanford: Stanford University Press, 2006, 109–36.

that is manifested in exclusion from the centres of economic, cultural and political power.[25]

Sociological analysis in terms of social class makes it possible to avoid reducing the study of inequality to the vertical and graded reading implied by scales of income or assets.[26] Aside from everything that separates social groups, internal divisions within social classes are equally crucial in the reconfiguration of inequality today. Within the working class, for example, the contrast between skilled workers, the proportion of whom is declining, and unskilled workers, on the rise owing to the expansion of the teritary sector, is accompanied by differences in class consciousness and in political and cultural participation. Among the middle class, even after the New Public Management turn that applies new rules to the public sector, there are still differences in conditions of employment between employees in the two sectors, which have repercussions in many other areas of social life. Differences in the arena of work are matched by differing cultural practices, values and political orientations, and by different lifestyles altogether.[27] Each 'big class' contains a large number of occupations, and this heterogeneity can obscure important divisions, but the 'microclass approach' cannot be clearly implemented at a European scale.[28]

What are the empirical bases for defining social classes? Some sociologists, following Marx, place the emphasis on position in the sphere of production, and hence on economic resources; others, on the basis of a rereading of Weber, focus on statutory position and

25    Olivier Schwartz, 'Does France Still Have a Class Society?', *Books and Ideas*, 3 March 2014, at booksandideas.net.

26    For a recent empirical proposal on this question, see Pirmin Fessler and Martin Schürz, 'The Functions of Wealth: Renters, Owners and Capitalists across Europe', Working Paper 223, Ostereichische National Bank, 2018.

27    Cédric Hugrée, Etienne Penissat and Alexis Spire, 'Differences between Public and Private Sector Employees Following the Managerial Turn in European States', trans. by Toby Matthews, *Revue française de sociologie (English Issue)* 56: 1, 2015, 47–73.

28    Kim A. Weeden and David B. Grusky, 'The Case for a New Class Map', *American Journal of Sociology* 111: 1, 2005, 141–212.

the signifiers of cultural and symbolic differentiation. In his work, Pierre Bourdieu attempted to combine these approaches, distinguishing class-fractions on the basis of their relative economic and cultural capital.[29] In this book, we draw on this multidimensional approach to describe the social space in Europe, taking the view that the term 'class' refers to the combination of economic and cultural capitals that construct both the socially and economically dominated positions of certain social groups and the forms of separation, distinction and cultural boundaries between them. The term can then be used as an overarching indicator of inequalities in standard of living (cultural practices, consumption, housing, access to health, etc.), employment and work. In statistical studies, this class position was for a long time measured in terms of individuals' occupation and employment status (employed or self-employed), in order to account for both their economic and their cultural resources. However, this representation of the social world has been subject to considerable criticism over the last twenty years.

Some writers point out that, in societies hit by unemployment and precarity, the crucial division is between insiders and outsiders, those included in and excluded from employment. Others, who take the view that occupation is increasingly less useful in explaining social behaviours, have developed more complex approaches based on multiple indicators. The British sociologist Mike Savage and his team, for example, suggest that individuals' financial resources, cultural practices (tastes in music, new technology practices, etc.) and their social capital (their network of relations) should be combined in a new analysis of class in the United Kingdom.[30] At the European level, it is not yet possible to reproduce this approach, since current statistical surveys do not

29   Pierre Bourdieu, *Distinction: A Social Critique of the Judgment of Taste*, Cambridge, MA: Harvard University Press, 1984; Loïc Wacquant, 'Symbolic Power and Group-Making: on Pierre Bourdieu's Reframing of Class', *Journal of Classical Sociology* 13:2, 2013, 274–91.

30   Mike Savage, with Niall Cunningham, Fiona Devine, Sam Friedman, Daniel Laurison, Lisa Mckenzie, Andrew Miles, Helene Snee and Paul Wakeling, *Social Class in the Twenty-First Century*, London: Pelican Books, 2015.

include questions that would allow these three types of capital to be measured. Moreover, assigning individuals to a given social class on the basis of their cultural practices (for example, the use of new technology) can tend to distinguish age groups – 'young' fans of hip hop and NICT (new information and communication technologies) as against 'older people' who love rock and are less comfortable with NICT – rather than social classes.

In fact, as recent studies show, occupation remains a useful tool for shedding new light on inequalities between citizens and their way of life.[31] It is still a determining factor, even when individuals have no job – or are no longer in formal employment. The unemployed vote, for example, is not homogeneous, and is linked much more to differences in social affiliation (most recent job), social origin (parents' profession) and level of education than to the fact of being unemployed. The same is true of pensioners, whose social practices remain largely determined by the position they held in the labour market.

## CLASSIFYING SOCIAL CLASSES

Assigning Europeans to a social class on the basis of their occupation is nevertheless still a risky business. It is debatable whether occupations can be equated – a French and a Hungarian nursing assistant, for example – when their characteristics (qualifications, position in the hierarchy, tasks undertaken) may vary from one country to another. In view of this, we use a classification of socio-economic groups in which occupations may be classified in slightly different ways in different countries: depending on the country, nurses may be classed among intellectual and scientific professions, or with associate professionals – but the social hierarchies

---

31  David Rose and Eric Harrison, *Social Class in Europe: An Introduction to the European Socio-economic Classification*, New York: Routledge, 2010; Daniel Oesch, *Redrawing the Class Map: Stratification and Institutions in Britain, Germany, Sweden and Switzerland*, New York: Palgrave Macmillan, 2006.

derived from these categories are similar across the different European countries.[32] The second problem is that European data on the most recent job held by unemployed people or by pensioners are usually lacking, with the result that our argument is necessarily based on people in work.[33] This restriction of the analysis to people in work under-represents the groups that are economically and socially most vulnerable,[34] but it offers an overarching frame of reference for social inequality that opens new avenues for research, particularly for observing the way in which class configurations are constructed in relation to the division of labour in Europe.

Moreover, thanks to two new sources of empirical data, it is now possible to make a statistical study of inequality in terms of class. First, the fact that European studies of employment and standard of living based on large samples have become stably established over the last ten years means that individuals' occupational status can be correlated with a whole range of indicators without losing the statistical representativeness of the results. Second, the standardised socio-economic classification for Europe, known as the European Socio-economic Groups (ESEG), devised in 2014 and adopted by Eurostat in 2016, has the virtue that it can be used in studies throughout Europe.[35]

This classification divides people who are in work into seven socio-economic groups and thirty subgroups. We use these as a basis for separating the European social space into three classes: the working class, the middle class and the dominant class. Besides being useful pedagogically, this tripartite division of the European social space is built by weaving together a conceptual approach to social class with the results of the various surveys on which we drew. The method by which these classes were identified (described

32    Cécile Brousse, 'L'Union européenne, un espace social unifié?', *Actes de la recherche en sciences sociales* 219, 2017, 12–41; Louis Chauvel, 'Existe-t-il un modèle européen de structure sociale?' *Revue de l'OFCE*, 71, 1999, 281–98.

33    See Appendix 1, 'Secondary Use of Four European Surveys'.

34    Will Atkinson, 'Rethinking the Work–Class Nexus: Theoretical Foundations for Recent Trends', *Sociology* 43: 5, 2009, 896–912.

35    INSEE, 'Eseg (European Socio-economic Groups): Nomenclature socio-économique européenne', Working Paper F 1604, 2016.

in Appendix 2) is based on observation of the income, qualifications, standard of living and conditions of employment and work
of the thirty socio-economic subgroups. The working class incorporates unskilled white-collar workers and manual workers
(cleaners, farm labourers, those employed in the retail and service
industries, etc.), skilled workers (those employed in craft; in the
food and drink industry; in construction, metallurgy and electronics; and drivers), nursing assistants, childcare workers, home-
care assistants, craftsmen and farmers. Those identified as
members of the middle class include shopkeepers; skilled white-
collar workers (office workers, police officers, receptionists, and
customer service clerks, etc.); associate professionals such as IT
engineers and technicians health associate professionals (for
example, nurses); finance, sales and administration associate
professionals (accountants, etc.), teachers, etc.; and self-employed
hotel and restaurant owners or managers. The dominant class
incorporates most of the intellectual and scientific professions
(doctors and healthcare specialists; managers in administration,
finance and business; engineers and specialists in science, engineering and information technology; lawyers and judges; journalists; artists; etc.), senior managers and CEOs.

In the French edition of the book, we use the plural to highlight
the internal diversity of these three major social classes. Here, we
chose the singular following the usual term in English. We take up
the expression 'working class', which refers to a broad social group
including blue-collar workers, unskilled employees and small-scale
self-employed. In the same way, we also use the expression 'middle
class' that includes the petty bourgeoisie and the lower middle class.
To identify the top of the European social space, we choose the term
'dominant class', which encompasses all workers who have the power
to impose rules in professional, social and even political life.[36]

---

36   Throughout the book, the term dominant class is used in reference
to Pierre Bourdieu's work, but it refers to a much broader group. It corresponds
to all social actors who have at least one type of capital – cultural, economic
or symbolic – that allows them to exercise domination in certain spheres of
the social space.

Combining the use of data from large-scale European statistical surveys with a division of the space into three social classes
makes it possible to sketch an initial response to questions that are
never posed in debates on Europe: how are inequalities of class
manifested in terms of physical strenuousness of work, unemployment and precarity, access to new technology, choice of place of
residence, housing conditions, cultural practices and access to
health? This set of factors can be used to piece together the jigsaw
of classes in Europe, and to understand the political movements
and splits that run through the continent.

# 1

# The Weakened Working Class

Since 2008, the eruption of the Greek debt and the crisis in public finance have exposed the marked disparities in economic development between different European countries. Despite the constantly reiterated promises that social policy would be standardised, the most disadvantaged groups in some countries have been hit much harder by the crisis than in others. During the 1990s, the received wisdom was that the social and economic structures of the countries comprising the European Union at that time would inevitably converge. Many sociologists have prophesied the inexorable disappearance of the working-class world, and its replacement by a large middle class. Thirty years later, social structure is far from uniform across European countries, and the working class has not disappeared.

However, the term 'working class' is singularly absent from most public debate about Europe. The European Commission prefers the terms 'poor' – those who earn less than 60 per cent of median wage[1] – or 'excluded' – all those who lack the means to meet their needs. In technocratic discourse, Europe is summed up as an opposition between 'insiders' and 'outsiders', with unemployment the main differentiating criterion used to measure inequality. By thus homogenising the 'bottom' of society, this approach conceals the relations of power and the social processes that are at the root of these subaltern positions. This binary perspective, dividing people into winners and losers under the new rules of the labour market, suggests that inequality can be reduced to differences between individual life

---

1　The median wage divides the total of wages into two equal sets: there are as many who earn more as there are who earn less.

paths. The concept of the working class helps to break with this representation of the world in terms of singular viewpoints and mobilities, for it reminds us that subaltern positions are inherited and reproduced.

In this chapter, we seek to highlight those factors that, beyond national citizenship, unite socio-economic groups as disparate as cleaners, manual workers, retail saleswomen, small tradespeople and farmers in order to shed light on the relations of power that operate throughout the continent. Identifying the common characteristics of the European working class is also a way of evaluating the effects the economic crisis has had on these social groups, by revealing their particular vulnerability, and emphasising the obstacles to trade union and political activism among these groups throughout Europe.

## PORTRAIT OF A SOCIAL GROUP IN
## COMPETITION THROUGHOUT EUROPE

In recent years, every effort has been made to bring the working classes of the different European countries into conflict with one another, exacerbating the competition arising from the globalisation of trade. Indeed, it is primarily the sectors employing large numbers of manual workers that have been displaced from the centre to the periphery or even beyond the margins of the continent. Chains of outsourcing also developed considerably during the 1990s, and have been strengthened in the East since the 2000s: more than 4.5 million employees in Europe work in an industrial enterprise whose activity is subcontracted by a company in another European country.[2] These movements have major consequences for the social situation within a number of companies that are particularly at risk, where job blackmail has become common currency: adjustments of working hours, wage cuts, productivity pushes and everything else become negotiable, even in the German automotive

---

2   Figures for 2014 from the World Industrial Subcontracting Show (Midest).

sector where the trade unions are still strong. Aside from these relocations, the fall in industrial employment in Western Europe is also due to a shift in the division of labour at the European level, mainly between the former Eastern countries and those of the North and West. This increasing specialisation of work between countries alters the shape and composition of social classes in Europe.

## The dream of a Europe without proletarians

According to the accepted doctrine currently operative in Brussels, the tertiarisation of the European economy is synonymous with an unstoppable march towards a Europe of the knowledge economy that will become the domain of managers and highly skilled professionals. Manual professions and unskilled jobs would be destined to disappear, through the development of robots and digital technologies that would replace workers carrying out unskilled tasks. In reality, nothing is less certain. Undoubtedly, since the 1970s, industry has been declining in importance in Europe, being replaced by new activities in retail, services, banking, etc. The tertiary sector (services and retail) is now the biggest employer, representing seven out of every ten jobs. This development has by no means led to the disappearance or even the minimisation of the working class in Europe. But the tertiarisation process has also changed low-skilled jobs. In fact, unskilled occupations and jobs have increased markedly at the same time, because these new services also require a workforce that can take on tasks where skill is less recognised. Moreover, the increase in women's levels of employment, and the ageing of the population in the North and West, create new needs in relation to childcare, care for the elderly and domestic tasks. Thus the number of domestic cleaners, childcare workers, home-care assistants, shopworkers, cashiers, sales assistants and nursing assistants (all jobs occupied predominantly by women) is increasing sharply all over Europe.[3] This has led some to

3   Daniel Oesch and Jorge Rodriguez Menes, 'Upgrading or Polarization? Occupational Change in Britain, Germany, Spain and Switzerland, 1990–2008', *Socio-Economic Review* 9: 3, 2011, 503–31; Camille Peugny, 'L'évolution de la structure sociale dans quinze pays européens (1993–2013): Quelle polarisation de l'emploi?', *Sociologie* 9: 4, 2018, 399–416.

conclude that a polarisation of European social structures is under way: on the one hand, highly skilled, well-paid employees and, on the other poorly skilled, low-paid precarious workers.[4]

But this polarisation is also related to patterns of specialisation and division of labour linked to globalisation. In the countries of the South of Europe and in Germany, the growth in unskilled occupations sits alongside a high number of skilled administrative workers. In most of the former countries of the East, the proportion of unskilled workers remains limited, while skilled manual workers still predominate. In Scandinavia, social-democratic governments have limited the decline in skilled work:[5] Finland and Denmark, for example, have seen a sharp rise in the number of skilled female manual workers. In addition to these national peculiarities, disparities persist in the different states' strategies of intervention. Over the last twenty years of the twentieth century, some social indicators (social-welfare expenditure, levels of employment) in the member states of the European Community have tended to converge, but this process has been interrupted by the successive expansions to incorporate new countries, and by the varying reactions to the crisis of 2008. Plans for reducing national debt, imposed under the Stability and Growth Pact, have been much more drastic in Ireland, in the countries of the South and in the former socialist countries. The proportion of young people under thirty who are inactive – not in education, employment or training – reveals a growing contrast between two groups of countries, with a European average of 16 per cent in 2013, and major disparities between nations. On one side, the level was around 8 per cent in the Netherlands, Denmark and Sweden; on the other, it was around 25 per cent in Italy, Greece and Bulgaria.[6] Underlying this

4  Maarten Goos, Alan Manning and Anna Salomons, 'Explaining Job Polarization: Routine-Biased Technological Change and Offshoring', *American Economic Review*, 104: 8, 2014, 2509–26.

5  Daniel Oesch, 'Welfare Regimes and Change in the Employment Structure: Britain, Denmark and Germany since 1990', *Journal of European Social Policy*, 25: 1, 2015, 94–110.

6  Marine Boisson-Cohen and Bruno Palier, 'Les trajectoires post-crise des pays de la zone Euro: Vers une dualisation économique et sociale de l'Europe', *Cahiers français*, 387, 2015, 16–22.

disparity there are differences in economic growth but also in social policy: the pressure from the European Union to reduce public spending is superficially comparable in each country, but not all states have the same capacity or the same desire to resist, as is manifested by the increasing national differences in expenditure on health, education, family support and unemployment benefit.

Thus the experience of unemployment and precarity may vary from one country to another, depending on the level of benefits and social protection established by the different states.[7]

### The two faces of European deindustrialisation

While deindustrialisation has led to the decline of manual labour in the six founding members of the European Union, this is not the case at the level of the twenty-seven countries that now make it up. In most Central and Eastern European countries and in the Baltic states, industrial production accounts for between 20 and 30 per cent of workers, compared with the European average of 18 per cent. This significant share held by industry is partly due to successive waves of relocation, especially in the automotive sector.

In the countries of the South, some regions which previously specialised in the textile industry, such as Tuscany or northern Portugal, have been hit hard by the departure of entire factories, speeding the decline of the manual sphere in these countries. Overall, the tertiary sector represents a comparable proportion of economic activity to that in the countries of the North and West, but this apparent equivalence is deceptive: these are activities mainly involving unskilled tertiary work, in sectors such as retail, transport and personal services.

Thus the years 1990–2000 were marked by a combination of a new division of production with the deterioration of conditions of employment in Europe. Differentiations within social structures were exacerbated by increased competition between workers. The working class was caught in a vice on both sides of the continent: on one side, those in the countries of the East and the South are forced

7   Duncan Gallie and Serge Paugam (eds.), *Welfare Regimes and the Experience of Unemployment in Europe*, Oxford: Oxford University Press, 2000.

to accept low wages or even to emigrate to find work; on the other, those in the North and West face company relocations and have to accept wage restraint and job flexibility in order to keep hold of the jobs that remain. This gives an idea of the social shock that has hit the whole of the continent, in the context of expansion of the European Union without any requirement for social convergence.

*Graph 1. The Employed Labour Force in European Countries by Sector of Activity.*

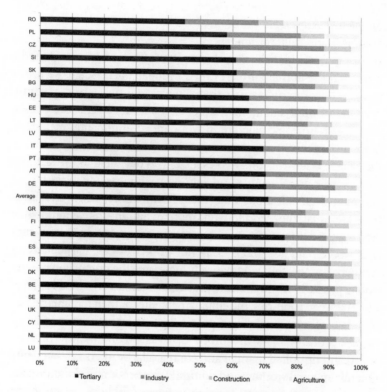

*Data*: LFS 2014. *Population*: Employed persons aged twenty-five to sixty-five, EU 27 (excluding Malta).

The countries of Europe can thus be divided into three large groups, on the basis of economic structure: in the West and North, skilled service jobs predominate; in the East, industrial jobs remain central; the South is characterised by the persistence of a traditional and unskilled tertiary sector. Finally, while little remains of the agricultural sector in the North and West (making up 1 per cent of jobs compared to an average of 5 per cent in Europe as a whole), it is holding firm in the countries on the margins of Europe, which are also the least developed: Greece, Romania, Poland, Lithuania, Latvia, Slovenia and Bulgaria. The former countries of the East and those of the South effectively constitute the workshop, the market garden and the breadbasket of countries in the North and West of Europe.

### Small-scale self-employed workers still present in substantial numbers

If we now consider the social characteristics and working conditions of those at the bottom of the European social scale, we find a number of common features that allow us to draw a group portrait.

One of these common features is that, on the European scale, working-class people who are in work are predominantly men: they make up 60 per cent of this group, compared to only 45 per cent among the middle class. This over-representation is due, first, to the fact that women who work tend, in all European countries, to have higher educational qualifications than men. Furthermore, where qualifications are equal, they tend to work more in administrative jobs, while men are predominant in manual or technical professions.[8] Working-class women are also more likely not to be in work, particularly in Southern Europe, thus automatically increasing the proportion of men among people in work. And although there may be considerable differences between countries, the employment rate for men remains higher than that for women in all European countries, without exception.

The working class in Europe consists predominantly of low-skilled and unskilled manual and white-collar workers (40 per cent) – mainly manual workers and domestic cleaners – and skilled workers (38 per cent), most of them in industry (Table 1). To these are added other, mainly female, occupations such as nursing assistants and childcare workers.

---

8   Thomas Amossé and Monique Meron, 'Le sexe des métiers en Europe', in Margaret Maruani (ed.), *Travail et genre dans le monde*, Paris: La Découverte, 2013, 269–78.

*Table 1. Socio-economic Groups within*
*the Working Class in Europe*

| Skilled white-collar workers (7%) | Nursing assistants, childcare workers and home-care assistants | 7% |
|---|---|---|
| Small-scale self-employed workers (15%) | Farmers | 7% |
| | Craftsmen | 8% |
| Skilled manual workers (38%) | Skilled construction workers | 6% |
| | Skilled craft or food and drink industry workers | 4% |
| | Workers in the metalwork and electronics industries | 12% |
| | Machine operators | 7% |
| | Drivers | 9% |
| Unskilled manual workers and white-collar workers (40%) | Retail and service assistants | 19% |
| | Manual labourers | 10% |
| | Cleaners | 9% |
| | Agricultural workers | 2% |
| Total of working class | | 100% |

*Source*: LFS 2014. *Population*: People in work aged between twenty-five and sixty-five, EU 27 (excluding Malta).

Over Europe as a whole, the proportion of self-employed workers – farmers and craftsmen – is fairly substantial. But this average masks wide disparities: in the regions of the East and South, being in paid work is far from the norm in all sectors, and a large number of the working class work for themselves. This situation contrasts strongly with that in France, the United Kingdom and Germany, for example, where the proportion of farmers is no more than 1 per cent.

But there should be no mistake: these small-scale self-employed workers have little in common with entrepreneurs who have several employees under their command. In most cases, they are sole craftsmen, sometimes supported by one or two employees: they are particularly exposed to the vagaries of the economy, and are in a weak position to borrow or to develop their enterprise. In Poland, four-fifths of farmers (around 2.8 million people) work on small farms (less than ten hectares) which earn them little (less than €3,000 per year). Such farms barely meet the needs of self-sufficiency, forcing both partners in the household to work on the land (mixed farming with cereals, sugar beet, potatoes, hay and pasture) and raise a few animals, while supplementing this income through other work.[9] The situation is similar, or even more difficult, in Romania, where three-quarters of farms occupy less than one hectare. Very often, these self-employed workers have no protection, and live in real social insecurity. Despite pressure from the European Union to subsidise only large farms, the Romanian authorities, particularly the Social Democratic Party, attempt to support small agricultural units, bypassing European norms in order to allow many working-class households to subsist – and thus secure their electoral support.[10]

In Greece, many self-employed people work for only one employer. These quasi-employees are, however, still registered with the social-security system as self-employed, and thus assume all the risks associated with the vagaries of the economic situation: they have no right to redundancy pay, or to unemployment benefit if their contract is terminated. In Spain, those known as 'autonomous workers' have gradually been granted social rights similar to those of employees, but they have been hit much harder by the economic crisis. In some sectors, such as transport, the self-employed lorry driver has to constantly increase his working hours in order to maintain his income, exposing him to the risk of legal sanction.[11] The result is permanent state of competition between self-employed and employed drivers, enabling the large haulage companies to eliminate all possibility of collective action.

9    François Bafoil, *Central and Eastern Europe: Europeanization and Social Change*, New York: Palgrave Macmillan, 2009.

10    Antoine Roger, 'Subversions locales et usages partisans des politiques européennes: L'exemple de la petite viticulture en Roumanie', *Politix* 83, 2008, 179–202.

11    Pablo López-Calle, 'L'autoexploitation au volant: Les camionneurs indépendants espagnols', *La nouvelle revue du travail* 8, 2016, 167–206.

Increasing competition can also be seen among employed working-class people, where the proportion of manual workers remains high, particularly in industry. This preponderance of manual work nevertheless has a new geographical distribution: many industrial jobs have been relocated from Western Europe to the margins, in the East and South. Poland offers a typical example. After it joined the European Union in 2004, the country became host to the factories of major electronics and white-goods manufacturers, mainly in the Warsaw region and in the south of the country. American computer manufacturer Dell, for example, closed its production site at Limerick, in Ireland, transferring it in January 2008 to a new plant in Łódź, Poland's third city. Poland has also become the largest manufacturer of flat screens in Europe. More recently, in January 2017, the Whirlpool group announced its decision to close its tumble-dryer plant in Amiens, in France, and relocate it to Poland, despite having received subsidies to modernise the French site. For the last twenty years these movements have contributed, bit by bit, to altering the profile of the working class in Europe.

Beyond the division between the self-employed and wage earners, what the working class has in common is that it is the group most exposed to international competition, through both migration and relocation.

## THE MAP OF THE WORKING CLASS IN EUROPE

The new distribution of production in Europe means that the relative proportion of the working class is far from uniform throughout the countries of the European Union. In broad outline, a contrast can once again be drawn between a Europe of the South and East, including the Baltic states, where the working class forms the largest proportion of the population, and a Europe of the North and West, where the middle class comprises a substantial share.

In one group of countries, then, the working class is predominant among people in work. This group comprises the southern periphery (Portugal, Spain, Greece) and the central and eastern periphery (the former socialist countries) of Europe (see Map 1). In these countries, the proportion of working-class people is higher than the European average (43 per cent), and considerably greater than that of other social classes.[12] In Romania they make up as much as two-thirds of the working population. Italy, Cyprus and Austria have a similar class structure: the proportion of working-class people is slightly above the European average, but the middle class is also large.

*Map 1. The Working Class in European Countries*

*Key*: Darker grey countries indicate a proportion of the working class in work greater than the EU mean; lighter grey indicates a proportion less than the EU mean. On average the working class represents 43 per cent of employed people, aged twenty-five to sixty-five, in Europe, EU 27 (excluding Malta). *Source*: LFS 2014.

---

12   See Table 15, appended 'ESEG classification (detailed level) and social class'.

In Central and Eastern Europe, but also in Portugal and particularly in Greece, a significant proportion of the working class works in agriculture, which remains low intensity. The basic type of farm is centred on the family unit and self-sufficiency: in Poland, these farms occupy 16 per cent of the cultivated land and employ 30 per cent of the agricultural workforce;[13] the proportions are very similar in Romania. In Spain, the agricultural sector still employs a large workforce – smaller nevertheless than in the former socialist countries – but in very different circumstances: it is highly dependent on immigrant labour, working on large mixed farms. In addition, temporary employment agencies in Spain provide the services of contract workers from Latin America and North Africa to farmers operating in other European countries, such as France. These workers are in principle affiliated to the Spanish social-welfare system, but in practice have no access to healthcare, and the company deducts from their wages the cost of travel between Spain and the countries where they work.[14]

In the countries of the former communist bloc, the transition to a market economy has often been brutal. It was accompanied by a rise in inequality throughout the 1990s and 2000s, to the advantage of a small minority usually concentrated in the capitals or the major cities. In some countries, such as the Czech Republic, the working class has, however, been relatively protected by the state during the transition from a planned economy to liberalism. Moreover, the Czech government encouraged the establishment of new industries, for example in the automotive sector where Škoda – the Soviet-era carmaker of Czechoslovakia – was bought by Volkswagen. This kind of change results in major disruption for suppliers: the parts manufacturer Valéo chose to end production in Spain because Volkswagen had relocated its Spanish plants to Slovakia, while at the same time the Czech Republic had supported

13   Bertrand Hervieu and François Purseigle, *Sociologie des mondes agricoles*, Paris: Armand Colin, 2013, 239.

14   Béatrice Mésini and Catherine Laurent, 'Concurrence des marchés de main-d'œuvre et dumping social dans l'agriculture', *Économie rurale* 349–50, 2015, 171–6.

the development of a network of subcontractors capable of collaborating closely with German constructors and parts manufacturers. However, the long-term unemployed and pensioners were less protected from the effects of the transition followed by the crisis.

Elsewhere, in all of the countries of the southern and eastern periphery, the working class was particularly badly hit by the 2008 financial and economic crisis. In the South this resulted in a huge rise in unemployment, particularly among young people, and increasing job insecurity. The result has been a resurgence in undeclared work, the level of which is probably much higher than elsewhere in Europe.[15] The former countries of the East and the Baltic states have also paid a heavy price for the crisis, which first took the form of a sharp increase in unemployment (except in the Czech Republic). Unemployment has fallen since 2011, although youth unemployment remains high in Poland, Romania and Slovakia. In the Baltic countries, many workers have had to combine two jobs, while in Poland and Slovenia the number of short-term contracts has risen sharply.[16] However, in this region of Europe adjustment to the crisis has principally taken the form of powerful wage restraint, with levels of low pay, and hence of poverty among workers, that are the highest in Europe.

Overall, this first group of countries of the southern and eastern periphery of Europe comprises, on one hand, the winners from liberalisation of the economy, who hold the monopoly on most of the economic, cultural and social resources, and, on the other, the large working class, who often survive by means of small underpaid jobs, meeting their daily needs through informal exchange networks of family and friends.

## *The working class: destination for migrants*
The working class in Europe is also characterised by the high proportion of immigrants among its numbers: it absorbs many

15   Mihail Hazans, 'Informal Workers across Europe: Evidence from 30 Countries', IZA discussion paper, Institute for the Study of Labor, 5871, 2011, doi.org.

16   André Cartapanis, Audrey Koulinsky and Nadine Richez-Battesti, 'L'hétérogénéité sociale de l'Union européenne après l'élargissement et la question des délocalisations', *Revue économique* 57: 4, 2006, 793–822.

more foreigners than all other social groups (Table 2). Contrary to popular belief, this represents the continuation of an age-old process, originating in the Middle Ages and tightly bound up with the development of capitalism and the wage system.[17]

*Table 2. Non-European Foreigners among the European Working Class*

|  |  | Proportion of non-European foreigners |
|---|---|---|
| Working class (6%) | Nursing assistants, childcare workers, home-care assistants | 7% |
|  | Farmers | 0.5% |
|  | Craftsmen | 4% |
|  | Skilled construction workers | 6% |
|  | Skilled craft or food and drink industry workers | 5% |
|  | Workers in the metalwork and electronics industries | 3% |
|  | Machine operators | 5% |
|  | Drivers | 4% |
|  | Retail and services assistants | 5% |
|  | Manual labourers | 9% |
|  | Cleaners | 16% |
|  | Agricultural labourers | 6% |
| Dominant class |  | 2% |
| Middle class |  | 2% |

*Source*: LFS 2014. *Population*: People in work aged between twenty-five and sixty-five, EU 27 (excluding Malta).

17   Yann Moulier-Boutang, *De l'esclavage au salariat: Economie historique du salariat bridé*, Paris: PUF, 1998.

Far from being confined to the richer countries, recourse to migrant workers is also common in the countries of Central and Eastern Europe. In Czech industry, for example, local employers called on foreign labour before the 2008 crisis, in order to meet labour shortages and particularly to counter the wage demands of workers in the large international firms such as Škoda (motor vehicles, Volkswagen group) and Foxconn (a Taiwanese electronics corporation). Usually working in unskilled sectors, immigrants are also more at risk of unemployment throughout Europe.

These results shed a different light on the discourse among European leaders about the dangers of xenophobia emerging from the 'lower levels' of society: unlike the dominant class, which is so ready to promote transnational mobility and tolerance of others, the working class is in fact much more mixed and mingled than all other social groups. The increase in cross-national marriages in Spain in the last fifteen years confirms this: the least skilled workers are the Spanish people most likely to marry a non-European foreigner, usually from Latin America, or a migrant from Central or Eastern Europe.[18]

In a period of crisis, this greater openness nevertheless manifests in competition on the labour market, leading to more powerful tensions and reactions among manual workers, low-skilled white-collar workers and farm labourers than among those higher up in the social hierarchy. These tensions sometimes limit the potential for mobilisation. In the United Kingdom, for example, the strategies of the unions seeking to mobilise migrants and local citizens together are tested severely by the wide range of different statuses of vulnerable workers. A recent campaign in the cleaning sector shows that it is sometimes difficult to bring together the concerns and demands of workers who have different status, depending on whether they are British, EU citizens or non-European foreigners, legally resident or

18   Juan Diez Medrano, Clara Cortina, Anna Safranoff and Teresa Castro Martín, 'Euromarriages in Spain: Recent Trends and Patterns in the Context of European Integration', *Population, Space and Place* 20: 2, 2014, 157–76.

undocumented.[19] The dilemma for the unions is, then, to know whether they should be incorporated into the campaign on the basis of their position in the organisation of labour, or of their legal status.

## SHARED VULNERABILITY IN THE EUROPEAN LABOUR MARKET

The increase in unemployment in Europe is often presented as afflicting all groups without distinction, but the effects of the crisis, of globalisation and of the spread of new technologies are not undifferentiated in the world of work: the working class is in the front line of this destabilisation of the labour market, making it more vulnerable than all other social groups.

*The working class in a position of social insecurity*
Unemployment does not affect Europeans at random: it has a more systematic impact on the lower end of the social hierarchy.[20] In 2011, three years after the start of the economic crisis in Europe, unemployment among the over-twenty-fives was on average 5 per cent, with wide disparities between social classes: the level was 11 per cent among the working class, compared to less than 3 per cent among the dominant class. Whereas only 3 per cent of executives experience unemployment, it affects 11 per cent of skilled workers and 14 per cent of unskilled manual and white-collar workers.[21] Moreover,

---

19   Gabriella Alberti, Jane Holgate and Maite Tapia, 'Organising Migrants as Workers or as Migrant Workers? Intersectionality, Trade Unions and Precarious Work', *International Journal of Human Resource Management*, 24: 22, 2013, 4132–48.

20   Duncan Gallie, Serge Paugam and Sheila Jacobs, 'Unemployment, Poverty and Social Isolation: Is There a Vicious Circle of Social Exclusion?', *European Societies*, 5: 1, 2003, 1–32.

21   The survey population does not include those unemployed people who could not be redeployed in their profession, and workers in those countries where this information was absent or incomplete (Ireland, Malta, France, the Netherlands, Slovenia, Romania). We used 2011 data and aggregated level of ESEG because the data are missing or very incomplete, depending on country, in the 2014 LFS survey.

for many households in working-class neighbourhoods, the risk of losing one's job is doubled, for it threatens both partners. This heightened risk of unemployment is accompanied in most European countries by drastic reductions in unemployment benefit, in the name of promoting an 'active' social state that makes any new benefit conditional on the individual taking steps to find work.[22]

*Table 3. Unemployment among Europeans*

|  | Unemployment rate |
| --- | --- |
| Managers | 3% |
| Intellectual and scientific professions | 3% |
| Intermediate professions | 4% |
| Self-employed workers | 4% |
| Skilled white-collar workers | 7% |
| Skilled manual workers | 11% |
| Unskilled manual and white-collar workers | 14% |
| Dominant class | 3% |
| Middle class | 5% |
| Working class | 11% |

*Source*: LFS 2011. *Population*: People in work aged between twenty-five and sixty-five, EU 27 (except for France, Ireland, the Netherlands, Romania, Slovenia, for which the rate of failure to provide ESEG-related unemployment data was over 30 per cent, and which were therefore excluded).

Hit by redundancies, an increase in long-term unemployment and the erosion of social protection, the European working class lives in uncertainty about the future: more than any other group, they fear losing their job within the next six months (+ 3 percentage points more than the average for Europeans overall).

---

22  Vincent Dubois, 'The Economic Vulgate of Welfare Reform: Elements for a Socioanthropological Critique', *Current Anthropology* 55: S9, 2014, 138–46.

But this fear of unemployment is not evenly spread throughout the working class: it is expressed by a quarter of skilled construction workers, 23 per cent of manual labourers and 22 per cent of farm labourers; among drivers, nursing assistants and childcare assistants, on the other hand, only 17 per cent fear losing their job, probably because many of the latter work in the public or quasi-public sector. Thirty years of successive relocations, initially within Europe, then throughout the world, have thus undermined manual workers' relationship with future employment, particularly among those who work directly with machines. For all of these people, the threat of unemployment is felt beyond the sphere of work: it feeds into a social vulnerability that taints their relationship with the future and produces a persistent but vague sense of abandonment, a process that leads them from being integrated in society to feeling themselves marginal.[23]

The working class's higher risk of unemployment is combined with a weaker status and a level of part-time employment higher than among other employed workers. In 2014 around 14 per cent of working-class people in employment had a temporary contract, compared to less than 9 per cent of the dominant and middle classes. Here again, there was a particularly sharp contrast between unskilled manual and white-collar workers, particularly manual labourers and farm labourers (17 per cent on temporary contracts), and senior managers (3 per cent). In most European countries, these insecure jobs are also the least well paid, regardless of age, level of education and sector, and women are those most likely to be employed in them.

Among women in employment, this precarity usually takes the form of part-time work. At the beginning of the 2010s, women predominated among part-time workers in Europe, whether under the pretext of adjustment of working hours or of flexibility.[24] At first sight, this gender inequality seems

23   Robert Castel, *From Manual Workers to Wage Laborers: Transformation of the Social Question*, New Brunswick: Transaction Publisher, 2003.

24   Margaret Maruani and Danièle Meulders, 'Genre et marché du travail dans l'Union européenne', in Maruani, *Travail et genre dans le monde*.

generalised: part-time work is equally common among the working class and the middle class. But this is only a superficial resemblance. Part-time work is twice as common among the working class as among the middle class, and particularly affects low-skilled women workers.

For these women, part-time work often prevents them from achieving an adequate standard of living, and forces them to find another source of income. The occupations where part-time work is most common are the least skilled: cleaners, childcare assistants, home-care assistants and domestic workers are now included in the sector of 'staff providing personal and household services'. Between 2008 and 2014, employment in this sector rose by 12 per cent, against a fall of 3 per cent in employment over all sectors during the same period.[25] At a time when the number of women in work is rising and the population ageing in every country in Europe, occupations involving domestic work (childcare, care for the elderly and domestic tasks) constitute a sector that is creating jobs, principally for women.

Whether they respond to a need or to a desire for comfort, these occupations now comprise one of the largest elements of the working class (except in the countries of Central and Eastern Europe). Some researchers see these caring professions ('care' for short) as a new marker of an increasingly globalised capitalism.[26] Thus the persistence of the patriarchal system – childcare, elderly care and domestic work are still predominantly the province of women – combined with the rising number of women in work in Western countries, particularly among more highly educated women, means that these tasks are taken on by working-class women who are very often immigrants or foreigners, and low-paid. In some countries, such as Germany and Austria, public

---

25    European Employment Policy Observatory (EEPO), *Thematic Review on Personal and Household Services*, European Commission, 2015, 4.

26    Arlie Russell Hochschild, 'Global Care Chains and Emotional Surplus Value', in Anthony Giddens and Will Hutton (eds.), *On the Edge: Living with Global Capitalism*, London: Jonathan Cape, 2000, 130–46.

policy has encouraged the employment of domestic staff on precarious contracts for low wages, reinforcing inequalities related to class and national origin among women.[27] Among cleaners, the proportion of non-European foreigners is 16 per cent, compared with an average of 6 per cent in the working class as a whole. In Austria, Spain, Estonia and Latvia, between 20 and 30 per cent of industrial cleaners are foreigners from outside Europe, and in Italy, Greece, Cyprus and Denmark the figure is between 30 and 65 per cent.

The working class as a whole is burdened by an accumulation of disadvantages that have intensified since the 2008 crisis: regular full-time work is increasingly less common, being replaced by hybrid forms of insecure jobs. The employers and the most liberal governments have taken advantage of the crisis to flexibilise the labour market, to the detriment primarily of manual workers and low-skilled white-collar workers. Rapid turnover, temporary contracts and part-time work have thus become the general rule, to the detriment of certain sections of the working class. Those particularly affected by unemployment and insecurity are women, non-European foreigners and young people. These destabilising factors prevent them from becoming integrated into the labour market and reduce the protection they are entitled to. Insecurity, moreover, is not confined to young people: unlike those in managerial and intermediate occupations, the working class is at risk of precarity at any age, including those aged over fifty. Job insecurity remains a constant in their working life.

*Onerous working conditions*
Working-class people in Europe are also those most likely to face hard and dangerous working conditions (Table 4). Contrary to popular belief, the technological advances of recent decades have not in fact put an end to the rigours of low-skilled and unskilled labour.

27   Karen Shire, 'Family Supports and Insecure Work: The Politics of Household Service Employment in Conservative Welfare Regimes', *Social Politics* 22: 2, 2015, 193–219.

*Table 4. Hardness of Working Conditions in Europe*

| 'Does your main job involve . . .?' | Repetitive hand or arm movements | Painful or tiring positions | Carrying or shifting heavy loads | Exposure to loud noise | Exposure to smoke or dust | Working standing up |
|---|---|---|---|---|---|---|
| Dominant class | 54% | 29% | 12% | 13% | 8% | 16% |
| Middle class | 52% | 32% | 17% | 20% | 9% | 23% |
| Working class | 71% | 58% | 50% | 38% | 24% | 65% |

*Source*: EWCS 2015. *Population*: People in work aged between twenty-five and sixty-five, EU 27 (excluding Malta). Note: onerous working conditions are usually defined as those in which survey respondents report being subject to them for at least one-quarter of their working hours. Those defined as working standing up are respondents who reported that their job 'never' or 'almost never' involved working sitting down.

For the vast majority of the working class in Europe, work involves 'repetitive hand and arm movements' (+ 20 percentage points more than in the middle class). To these are added 'painful or tiring positions', which are much more rarely encountered in other occupations. There are significant class differences in physical hardness of work in terms of jobs that involve regularly carrying heavy loads, regular exposure to loud noise or to smoke and dust, and those that involve working standing up. A number of occupational groups are particularly affected: half of all machine operators work exclusively with repetitive hand and arm movements; a quarter of skilled construction workers report working all or almost all of the time in painful or tiring working positions; a quarter of manual labourers state that they routinely have to carry heavy loads. These factors particularly affect workers in the metalwork and electronics industries, whose working conditions are much more onerous than those in the service industry, and who continue to suffer physically stressful working conditions as they get older. Small-scale self-employed workers are not exempt: they also have to carry heavy loads, and are relatively likely to be exposed to dust and smoke and to loud noise.

Working-class women seem to suffer less from some forms of harsh working conditions associated with industrial labour. For example, they are less often exposed to smoke or dust. However, they experience other forms of physical hardship, such as shifting heavy loads. The majority of cleaners, nursing assistants and child-care assistants have to remain standing for virtually the whole of their working day. Overall, 70 per cent of working-class women in Europe report that their work never or almost never involves working sitting down; this is the case for only 20 per cent of dominant and middle-class women.

Being regularly subject to the hardest working conditions significantly affects the relationship that working-class people have with their professional future: only two-thirds of them think they will be able to do the same work when they are sixty, compared to more than four-fifths of the dominant class. While this proportion is roughly equal between men and women, it varies markedly with age. Young people are more likely to anticipate being worn down by work: among the working class, a little of over half of those aged under thirty-five state that they would be able to do the same work at sixty, compared to three-quarters of those aged over fifty. This disparity relates both to socialisation at work and to changes in people's relation to the future over the course of their lives. The disenchantment born of a difficult start to working life in manual or unskilled jobs prevents people from imagining that they might continue in this work for many years. By contrast, once past a certain age, the fear of redundancy can make working conditions that younger people find intolerable seem acceptable.

The working class occupies a subordinate position in the labour market, which is manifested in an accumulation of disadvantages that vary depending on gender. In simplified terms, on the one hand are men who work in farming, skilled manual work and crafts, whose working conditions are physically the hardest, involving exposure to painful positions, loud noise, heavy loads, dust, smoke, vapour and repetitive hand and arm movements. On the other are the female cleaners, retail and service assistants, nursing assistants and childcare workers who tend more to work standing up in insecure jobs.

## A disadvantageous relation of power: the decline of unions and labour activism

Over the last forty years, the combination of unemployment and increasing job insecurity has had many repercussions on the working class's individual and collective capacities for resistance. This has resulted in a fall in activism, against a background of increasing intensity of labour. The concomitant decrease in levels of trade union affiliation and in the number of strike days is both the cause and the illustration of a balance of power that has shifted strongly to the disadvantage of the working class.

Continent-wide, in 2015 only 11 per cent of European workers stated that they were active in unions or political organisations, with marked variations between social groups: 15 per cent of the dominant class, 13 per cent among the middle class and 9 per cent among the working class. Within the working class, trade union or political activism remains more common among more skilled groups. Those most involved are skilled workers in the metalwork and electronics industries (13 per cent) and drivers and machine operators (11 per cent), while the proportion falls to 5 per cent among cleaners and skilled workers in craft and in the food and drink industry.

The quantification of 'political and trade union activity' on the European level is imprecise, and this broad view needs to be supplemented by figures on union membership. In all countries, except for the Scandinavian countries (Finland, Sweden and Denmark), Belgium and Spain, levels of union membership fell overall in Europe between the early 1980s and the 2000s.[28] The picture in individual nations varies widely, owing to the fundamentally different systems of industrial relations. In countries

---

28   Steen Scheuer, 'Union Membership Variation in Europe: A Ten-Country Comparative Analysis', *European Journal of Industrial Relations* 17: 1, 2011, 57–73.

where the unions have responsibility for services such as unemployment compensation (Scandinavian countries, Belgium), union membership has remained very high, and even increased, since belonging to a union is a way of ensuring priority access to support. In Belgium, for example, the unions are members of the organisations that pay unemployment benefits, and thus serve as intermediaries with the National Employment Office.[29] By contrast, in countries where union activity centres on mobilisation of workers (France, the United Kingdom, Italy, etc.), the erosion of membership has played a major role in shifts in the power relation with employers, particularly since many governments – following the British example – have fostered this shift by passing laws limiting workers' right to protest. In Spain, three general strikes were organised between 2010 and 2012 in opposition to reforms aimed at flexibilising the labour market, but faced with the government's refusal to back down, the unions changed strategy and broadened the campaign to the whole of the population,[30] with the risk that demands relating to the world of work became lost amid wider protest movements.

The socio-economic groups organised by the unions have altered substantially, in line with economic changes. Trade union presence in the industrial sector has declined, and unions still have difficulty gaining a foothold in services and retail, where the number of low-skilled jobs has risen. In Germany, campaigning activity has shifted from the manufacturing sector to the service sector, but this development has not checked the crisis in union representation.[31] In the public sector and in major corporations where employment is more secure, the unions are stronger; employees are represented by one or more organisations, whereas

29   Philippe Askenazy, *The Blind Decades: Employment and Growth in France, 1974–2014*, Oakland: University of California Press, 2014.

30   Oscar Molina and Oriol Barranco, 'Trade Union Strategies to Enhance Strike Effectiveness in Italy and Spain', *Transfer: European Review of Labour and Research* 22: 3, 2016, 383–99.

31   Heiner Dribbusch, 'Organizing through Conflict: Exploring the Relationship between Strikes and Union Membership in Germany', *Transfer: European Review of Labour and Research* 22: 3, 2016, 347–65.

this is rarely the case in the small and medium enterprises that make up an increasing proportion of European economies, owing to the growth in outsourcing. In addition, European employers have introduced many anti-union measures (blacklists of union activists, wrongful dismissals, wage discrimination, in-house unions, legal guerrilla tactics, the obstruction of union rights, etc.), backed by a flourishing market in consultants who specialise in discouraging activism. Thus a growing proportion of the working class has never been, or is no longer, represented in the workplace by a trade union.

This disadvantageous relation of power has repercussions on the capacity of the working class to mount protest actions. The legal regulations governing strikes vary from one country to another, and there is as yet no standard method for counting strike days.[32] The fact remains that in the majority of European countries, the number of strike days per employee has been falling since the late 1980s.[33] While a number of campaigns against factory closures and restructuring have hit the headlines (Arcelor-Mittal and Peugeot in France, Caterpillar in Belgium, Thyssen-Krupp's AST steelworks in Italy, etc.), many redundancy plans have been made behind closed doors, with limited resistance. Mass strikes have shifted from private industry to the public and transport sectors. In retail, job insecurity severely limits social activism, despite a few exceptions such as the campaign by the cleaners of luxury hotels in Paris, Uber and Deliveroo delivery staff in the United Kingdom, and Amazon employees in Germany.[34] The situation varies from

32   Wiebke Warneck, *Strikes Rules in EU 27 and Beyond*, Brussels: European Trade Union Institute for Research, Education and Health and Safety (ETUI-REHS), 2007.

33   Steen Scheuer, 'A Novel Calculus? Institutional Change, Globalization and Industrial Conflict in Europe', *European Journal of Industrial Relations* 12: 2, 2006, 143–64; Kurt Vandaele, 'Sustaining or Abandoning Social Peace? Strike Developments and Trends in Europe since the 1990s', working paper, ETUI, 2011.

34   Olivier Giraud and Michel Lallement, 'Les conflits du travail en Allemagne: Nouvelles formes, nouveaux enjeux', *Critique internationale* 65: 4, 2014, 65–83.

country to country, depending on the social balance of power and legislation relating to the right to strike. In France, the level of conflict remains high, but is manifested in fragmented and isolated campaigns.[35] In the United Kingdom, on the other hand, legal restrictions on the right to strike and the weakening of the trade unions make recourse to this kind of action very rare.[36] There are still more strikes in the countries of Western Europe, despite the fact that workers in some former countries of the East, such as the Czech Republic, have mounted strong campaigns against the liberal reforms and austerity policies imposed by their government. But these campaigns have largely involved public-sector employees, and the process of relocation of industry to these countries has not revived worker activism, except in a few exceptional cases such as the strike that broke out in the Dacia factories (a subsidiary of the Renault group) in Romania in March 2008.

The decline in union activism has paved the way for the implementation of policies aimed at deregulating employment rights, often at the instigation of the European Union. These changes primarily affect low-skilled and unskilled jobs in industry and services. For example, the European directive on working hours sets the maximum number of hours to be worked per week at forty-eight – and even at sixty hours under certain conditions for lorry drivers.[37] These 'minimum rules' are transposed to the various legislative systems of European states, but with upper limits set so high that labour legislation can vary widely from one country to another. In Poland, companies can now make greater demands for overtime or night working. In Portugal, overtime pay has been revised downwards. In the Czech Republic, Spain, Greece, Poland

---

35   Sophie Béroud, Jean-Michel Denis, Guillaume Desage, Baptiste Giraud and Jérôme Pélisse, *La lutte continue? Les conflits du travail dans la France contemporaine*, Bellecombe-en-Bauges: Le Croquant, 2008.

36   Thomas Amossé, Alex Bryson, John Forth and Héloïse Petit (eds.), *Comparative Workplace Employment Relations: An Analysis of Practice in Britain and France*, London: Palgrave Macmillan, 2016.

37   See directives 2003/88/CE and 2002/15/CE from the European Parliament and the Council of Europe, relating to adjustment of working hours.

and Romania, the maximum length of short-term contracts has been extended, and new types of work contract with fewer protections have been introduced. Finally, in the Czech Republic and Poland, redundancy pay has been cut, and in Slovakia the minimum notice period has been reduced.[38] And the European Union is continuing to demand that member states pass reforms imposing ever-increasing flexibility on the part of employees.

## INCOME AND CONSUMPTION: THE WORKING CLASS SPLIT IN TWO

While the working class in Europe has been severely weakened on the labour market, its situation in terms of level of resources and access to consumer goods gives less cause for concern, particularly compared to their peers in other parts of the world. Moreover, over the last decade, the level of education has risen throughout Europe, helping to bring the cultural practices of the different social groups closer together. Nevertheless, substantial inequalities remain, both in the financial domain and in access to leisure.

### Low-income families

A first measure of relative position in the social hierarchy is household disposable income: 22 per cent of the working class in Europe lives below the poverty line, meaning that members of it earn less than 60 per cent of the median wage in their country. This is due to the increase in unemployment, which forces more and more households to depend on a single source of income, and to wage-restraint policies. For these groups, deprivation is evident in every area of daily life. Those most at risk are farmers (40 per cent living below the poverty line), small-scale self-employed workers (29 per cent), low-skilled manual and white-collar workers (24 per cent) and farm labourers (23 per cent). These results offer a glimpse of the financial deprivation of whole swathes of the European working class, particularly in the countries of the South and East of Europe, where

---

38   European Trade Union Institute, 'Workers' Rights, Worker Mobilization and Workers' Voice', in Benchmarking Working Europe 2013, 90.

a class of small subsistence farmers, together with small-scale retail and craft sectors, persists. The financial subordination of the European working class emerges more clearly still when the composition of households is taken into account (Table 5).

Table 5. Poverty among European Households

|  |  | Proportion of individuals belonging to a family living below the poverty line |
|---|---|---|
| Working class | Lone parent with one or more dependent children | 41% |
|  | Two adults with three or more dependent children | 38% |
|  | Two adults with two dependent children | 23% |
|  | Two adults with one dependent child | 19% |
| Middle class | Lone parent with one or more dependent children | 19% |
|  | Two adults with three or more dependent children | 10% |
|  | Two adults with two dependent children | 7% |
|  | Two adults with one dependent child | 6% |

Source: EU-SILC 2014. Population: People in work aged between twenty-five and sixty-five, EU 27 (excluding Malta and Slovenia). Interpretation: 41 per cent of working-class people belonging to a household comprising a lone parent with several dependent children live below the poverty line in their country.

Working-class households in Europe are those most at risk of falling into financial poverty, but those with dependent children fare still worse. Those most affected by poverty are single women with children, the number of whom has increased markedly in the countries of Northern and Western Europe. An ethnographic survey conducted in a large social housing neighbourhood in Nottingham, in the East Midlands, revealed the mechanisms leading to such situations of poverty in the United Kingdom.[39] Against a background of deindustrialisation, men, primarily the descendants of Jamaican immigrant workers, are turning to the drug economy and therefore tend to be absent from the home either because they have to be constantly travelling or because they are in prison. Forced to accept precarious jobs in order to meet the needs of their family, women are in the front line of attacks from the social services and public authorities, who accuse them of living on welfare. The exclusion of these women is reinforced by austerity policies, and their children (who are often mixed-race) and their black partners suffer institutionalised racial discrimination, particularly at the hands of the police. The combination of these factors contributes to their becoming confined to their neighbourhood, which becomes the only place where they are safe from symbolic attacks and discrimination.

The financial vulnerability of the working class can be qualified with reference to inequalities in assets. Overall, self-employed workers tend to have more resources than employees, but these small variations are difficult to document over the whole of Europe. Moreover, limiting consideration merely to the financial dimension fails to take into account other forms of exclusion. In order to gain a more reliable representation of social inequality, the picture needs to be supplemented with information on access to certain consumer goods, and hence to cultural, symbolic and physical resources.

### Access to consumer goods: inequalities between countries, inequalities between social groups

In the domain of consumer goods, the European working class has a basic standard of living, but with differences between social groups. For example, 80 per cent of working-class people in Europe own a car, but car ownership is often lower among cleaners and

---

39   Lisa McKenzie, *Getting By: Estates, Class and Culture in Austerity Britain*, Bristol: Policy Press, 2015.

manual labourers (72 per cent) than among skilled workers in the metalwork and electronics industries (86 per cent). The divergences between countries are wider: only 41 per cent of working-class households in Romania, and 57 per cent in Hungary, state that they own a car, compared to 90 per cent of working-class households in France.

Access to holidays is another useful indicator of financial inequality between Europeans: half of the working class states that it cannot afford one week's holiday a year. Skilled workers in the metalwork and electronics industries are the working-class people most able to take a few days' holiday a year, while farmers and cleaners are the two categories most often lacking: 60 per cent of them never go on holiday. Rather than indicating affluence, this statistic reveals the difficulties that many people in Europe encounter in getting out of an everyday routine characterised by powerful occupational and financial constraints. The generalisation of part-time work and the deregulation of working hours make it difficult to plan leave. In this respect, the lack of holidays has a significance well beyond the confines of leisure: it is part and parcel of a more general shift that tends to confine the working class within national boundaries – except in the case of migration for work.

### The digital divide: financial or cultural boundary?

Computer ownership, a further indicator of access to consumer goods, is now widespread throughout Europe: nine Europeans in ten own a computer. The price of computers has fallen markedly, making them accessible to many consumers. And indeed, most (80 per cent) of the working class owns one, although in this domain, too, they are less well off than others.

Their likelihood of having access to digital technology still varies, however. Skilled workers, and white-collar employees in retail and services, are almost as well equipped as the average European. However, working-class people living in the countryside lag behind in this area: only seven out of ten farmers or agricultural labourers own a computer. Among the working class, levels of computer ownership are lower in the countries of Central and Eastern Europe, and in Portugal. Thus access to digital technology depends not only on income, but also on occupational status and geographical location. The reasons given by respondents for not having a computer are usually other than financial ones, because they do not feel the need for one, or do not feel comfortable with information technology.

The digital divide in effect owes as much to unequal grasp of IT skills as to difficulty accessing a computer or the Internet. More than two-thirds of Europeans state that they have a good understanding of new information and communication technologies (NICT),[40] a definition that encompasses the ability to use word processing and calculation software; to copy, save and compress files; to connect a peripheral device; to change software parameters; etc. The proportion is somewhat lower with regard to navigating the Internet, which includes using search engines, sending email, downloading and sharing files, posting messages on sites and forums, and so on. But these figures hide major inequalities. While a little under half of working-class people have a good grasp of new technology, more than four-fifths of middle-class people, and more than nine-tenths of the dominant class, say they do. Similarly, a little under half of working-class people know how to use the Internet, compared to three-quarters of the middle class and four-fifths of the dominant class.

Those who have greatest difficulty with new technology and the Internet are farmers, cleaners, farm labourers, manual labourers and skilled workers in craft, or in the food and drink industry or in construction. At the other end of the scale, executives and most of those working in intellectual and scientific professions have full grasp of NICT and the Internet. The middle class report very similar levels of competence, with the exception of shopkeepers, more than 40 per cent of whom have difficulty with these tools. These disparities in new technology skills to a considerable degree reflect the unequal importance of information technology in different occupations: those who use computers in their

---

40   Owing to a high level of non-responses, the United Kingdom is excluded from this indicator of NICT use; Ireland, Denmark and the Netherlands are excluded from the indicator of Internet use. See Appendix 1.

day-to-day work are most likely to be able to take full advantage of it at home. But these inequalities are also due to levels of skill and qualification: working-class people with the lowest educational qualifications are those least able to access these technologies. They suffer a double handicap as a result: first, on the labour market, because knowledge of these tools has become imperative even in jobs at the bottom of the social scale, and second, in terms of access to rights, since the development of an administration without counter service and the progressive move to electronic services places users less comfortable with text and computers at a disadvantage.[41]

Inequalities in grasp of technology are also linked to gender and age, two criteria that create greater discrimination at the bottom of the social scale. The gap between working-class men and women is 8 percentage points, and the generation gap is wider still: more than 70 per cent of those aged between twenty-five and thirty-five have a good grasp of information technology, compared to about 32 per cent of the oldest group (aged fifty and over). These divisions also pertain in the dominant and middle classes, but to a much lesser extent.

In a Europe where physically present staff are disappearing from public services, new technology could alleviate geographical and generational disparities, but in fact many indicators show that it usually reinforces phenomena of exclusion.

### Health inequality and going without treatment

While, in comparison to other regions of the world, it may appear that in Europe social-welfare systems enable the majority to access a basic level of care, there are nevertheless marked inequalities in the arena of health between different social groups. Here, the disadvantaged position of the working class is due primarily to their living and working conditions: exposure to pollution, work-related cancers and premature death vary according to occupation and place of residence. The risks related to asbestos for manual

---

41   Aurélien Buffat, 'Street-Level Bureaucracy and E-Government', *Public Management Review*, 17: 1, 2015, 149–61.

workers, and to pesticides for farm workers, offer two examples. To these need to be added all the deleterious effects on health of harsh working conditions: restricted capacity for work, chronic illness, and the feeling of being in poor health, particularly among older workers.[42] Vulnerability to unemployment and job insecurity also has serious effects on health.[43] These work-related social inequalities nevertheless vary considerably from one country to another, owing to the lack of common European legislation.

In Greece, for example, the financial crisis and austerity programmes have only increased these inequalities, by substantially reducing access to care and undermining the health of the population. The drastic financial measures imposed by the European Union reduced public health expenditure to the strict minimum, the effect of which was to withdraw social protection from the most vulnerable groups. This resulted in an increasingly unequal system of access to care, whereas before the crisis the entire population benefited from health insurance. More generally, since the 2008 crisis in public finance, many countries have increased the share of costs that patients have to pay, resulting in an increase in health inequality across Europe.

Overall, inequality in access to healthcare relates mainly to income and educational qualifications: this explains the disadvantaged position of working-class people, 9 per cent of whom, on a Europe-wide level, stated that they had had to forgo a medical appointment during the previous year. Eleven per cent of working-class people have already given up dental care, compared to only 6 per cent of middle-class people and 5 per cent of dominant-class people. These figures, however, contain some bias, as the definition of doing without care may vary depending on the importance attached to prevention and the necessity of looking after oneself.

---

42  Thierry Debrand and Pascal Lengagne, 'Pénibilité au travail et santé des séniors en Europe', *Économie et statistique* 403, 2007, 19–38.

43  David Rose and David Pevalin, 'Social Class Differences in Mortality using NS-SEC – Too Little Too Soon: A Reply to Chandola', *Social Science and Medicine* 51: 7, 2000, 1121–7.

Among the working class, 38 per cent of those who had gone without healthcare had done so for financial reasons (compared to 12 per cent among the dominant class), but many had gone without treatment for other reasons: because they did not have the time (16 per cent, compared to 30 per cent in the dominant class), because they hoped they would get better without taking anything (18 per cent), or because the waiting list was too long (14 per cent, compared to 22 per cent in the dominant class). This range of reasons shows that going without healthcare is far from an exclusively financial consideration: it relates to forms of self-censorship that need to be analysed in terms of class, not just income bracket. There may be reasons related to awareness of the need to look after oneself, to the availability of information, to the possibility of accessing specialist medical treatment, and to geographical isolation, particularly in rural and periurban areas. All of these obstacles combine to contribute to deepening social inequality in relation to mortality. The highest mortality rates are found among low-skilled workers, with managerial staff at the least risk, and this contrast is observed in all European countries.[44]

Income, consumption, access to information technology and health: these various domains of social life offer a glimpse of how the European working class split into two distinct groups. On one side are small-scale self-employed workers, mainly farmers, and low-skilled and proletarianised manual and white-collar workers. They often live below the poverty line, report that they find the end of the month difficult, and more often have difficulty accessing healthcare. They constitute the disadvantaged section of the working class. On the other side, skilled workers in the metallurgy and electronics industries, drivers, machine operators, and nursing and childcare assistants have greater access to everyday consumer goods such as

44  Adrienne E. Cavelaars, Anton E. Kunst, José W. Geurts, Uwe Helmert, Olle Lundberg, Andreas Mielck, Jil Matheson, Arié Mizrahi, Niels Kr. Rasmussen, Thomas Spuhler and Johan P. Mackenbach, 'Morbidity Differences by Occupational Class among Men in Seven European Countries: An Application of the Erikson–Goldthorpe Social Class Schema', *International Journal of Epidemiology* 27: 2, 1998, 222–30.

cars, holidays and computers. This split in the working class does not follow national boundaries: it is common throughout Europe, though it may be more or less marked depending on the country.

## CONCLUSION

Nevertheless, the crisis has hit the entirety of the working class in Europe with full force: unemployment and insecurity are part of their everyday experience and mark them out from other classes. Another recurrent feature is the physical hardness of their work – which affects low-skilled and unskilled workers the most – in almost all European countries. Yet little political attention has been paid to these inequalities in work. As concerns about working conditions have been relegated to an increasingly marginal space, the growing insecurity of the working class has been concealed. This insecurity takes the form of financial vulnerability, expressed sometimes as destitution, sometimes as precarity and social insecurity; it is also manifested in 'subordination in the division of labour and in political and social relations', and in deprivation of a range of cultural resources – whether these relate to new information and communication technologies, healthcare or lack of skills in foreign languages.[45] All of these markers of domination point to forms of social and cultural separation that define the contemporary working class. In this sense, the concept of class retains all its relevance.

We should add that, with those at the bottom of the hierarchy being systematically set in competition with one another, the process of their political marginalisation is exacerbated. This division helps to explain why some sections of the working class have ceased believing in the possibility of workers emancipating themselves, why others ally themselves with protectionist small-scale employers within national boundaries, and why others still cling

45   On the way in which these resources are unequally distributed between the dominant class and the working class, see Chapter 3 below. Olivier Schwartz, 'Does France Still Have a Class Society?', *Books and Ideas*, 3 March 2014, at booksandideas.net. Cf. note 25.

on to the idea of a possible alliance with the middle class. If they are unable to identify a common outlook, the risk is that they will withdraw from political activity. For a long time now, the working class has been under-represented among parliamentarians in the countries of the European Union, and this exclusion is reinforced by a retreat from the electoral arena: abstention rates are much higher among working-class people than among employers and managerial staff.[46] In short, the entire base of the social hierarchy is excluded from political life.

46 Aina Gallego, 'Unequal Political Participation in Europe', *International Journal of Sociology* 37: 4, 2007, 10–25.

# 2

# Delusions of Grandeur and Social Realities: The Middle Class

For more than a century, the middle class has been at the centre of European political debate, though the way this category is defined varies markedly from country to country.[1] Without giving it either specific sociological content or a clear sociological outline, political actors primarily perceive this social group as a means through which they can address the whole of society. Given that most people identify themselves, often wrongly, as middle-class, all sorts of misconceptions are thus possible. In Western Europe, the middle class is inextricably linked to a comprehensive social-welfare system and to the dream of a more equal society. After the fall of the Berlin Wall, in the former socialist countries, the middle class replaced the working class as a guarantor of social stability and a category with which people identified themselves.

The success of the term 'middle class', now dominant throughout the continent, is thus a function of its political usefulness. Many political leaders use the notion of the middle class to support a vision of a peaceful society devoid of class and other conflicts. The diametric opposition between the people and the elite is deemed to have been erased by the emergence of an intermediate class which, as it continues to grow, will come to represent society as a whole. Having become so widespread, this notion thus often operates as a means of disguising the disengagement of the working class and of passing in silence over the hegemony of the dominant class. Notwithstanding

---

1 Jürgen Kocka, 'The Middle Classes in Europe', *Journal of Modern History* 67: 4, 1995, 783–806.

this skilfully maintained vagueness, there is a need to establish the defining criteria for this group, which is consistently placed at the heart of the discourse around the prospects for social change.

When assessing social class, economists and European institutions use the income variable: they place the middle class between the bottom 20 per cent (the poor) and the top 20 per cent (the rich) of the distribution, corresponding therefore to the middle 60 per cent. Thomas Piketty has proposed an alternative distribution which he perceives as more in line with the reality of these social groups. He places the middle class between the poorest 50 per cent (the lower class) and the wealthiest 10 per cent (the upper class).[2] In both cases, however, this arithmetical approach to inequality reduces social hierarchy to the criterion of financial wealth alone and fails to take into account the role played by working conditions and the significance of cultural capital, two factors which are also sources of inequality. Moreover, while income may appear sufficient to compare wealth distribution in all countries over all eras, it is actually less precise than it seems at first sight. In most European countries, unearned income is underestimated to varying degrees, depending on the extent of the tax administration's influence on the economic fabric. In addition, data on property values and the income they generate are still difficult to collect at the European level.

Viewed in terms of position in the organisation of labour, the concept 'middle class' refers to disparate professional and social realities ranging from hotel managers to health associate professionals, including military non-commissioned officers and teachers. Senior managers, on the other hand, are not considered middle-class but rather as members of the dominant class (see Chapter 3). At first sight, this group, which represents 38 per cent of employed people in Europe, appears heterogeneous. But we cannot reduce the middle class to this image of a vague intermediate group defined simply in contrast to the two extremes of the social scale: neither poor nor rich, neither highly educated nor excluded from the 'race for degrees'. Depending on context and country, this class may be associated with the dominant class or

2   Piketty, *Capital in the Twenty-First Century*, 390–1.

with the working class. By shifting the electoral balance, the middle class can have a decisive impact on the balance of political power.

## THE MIDDLE CLASS AT WORK

Being essentially articulated through political discourse, the middle class is particularly difficult to define. One of its main features is not so much that it is in the middle of the social structure but rather that it acts as an interface between the working class and the dominant class (Table 6). Up to 25 per cent of the employed middle class state that they supervise subordinates, some of whom belong to the working class and others to the middle class.[3] This is particularly true for managers in shops, hotels and restaurants, as well as for non-commissioned officers and science, engineering and ICT technicians. The other important characteristic of the middle class is that its members are often in contact with the public in the context of administrative, retail, healthcare or teaching services. These day-to-day relationships with the public are neither standardised nor symmetrical, which means there is often a social and cultural distance from members of other social classes. Depending on the type of service and the financial and cultural resources of the public in question, members of these professions thus find themselves acting as advisers, even arbitrators, but also as subordinates.

### The old and new middle class of the old continent

Since the early years of this century, technological development has led to a sharp rise in the numbers of managerial staff and associate professionals, replacing a substantial proportion of the intermediate-level jobs lost through technological innovation and industry relocations. The technological revolution has contributed, for example, to a huge rise in the number of IT specialists in Europe, especially in the countries of the South and the former socialist

---

3   Behind this dividing line lies a gendered division of labour. In Europe as a whole, in the middle class one in four men, compared to only one in six women, has a supervisory role.

countries, where companies have bought heavily into new technology and have had to modernise. The financialisation of economies, and the increase in international trade, have also led to the proliferation of jobs for sales representatives, real-estate agents, brokers and insurance agents.

*Table 6. Socio-economic Groups within the Middle Class in Europe*

| | |
|---|---|
| Self-employed hotel and restaurant owners | 2% |
| Shop, hotel and restaurant managers | 2% |
| Teachers | 14% |
| Science, engineering and ICT technicians | 11% |
| Health associate professionals (e.g. nurses) | 7% |
| Sales and administration associate professionals (accountants, etc.) | 16% |
| Legal and social associate professionals | 4% |
| Non-commissioned officers in the armed forces | 0.5% |
| Shopkeepers | 13% |
| Office workers | 20% |
| Receptionists and customer service clerks | 5.5% |
| Police officers, armed service personnel and security agents | 5% |
| Total middle class | 100% |

*Source*: LFS 2014. *Population*: People in work aged between twenty-five and sixty-five, EU 27 (excluding Malta).

This expansion of the socio-economic structure in the middle and upper layers of society is not restricted to those areas subject to international competition. Despite the decline in the public sector, employment in public services, particularly education and health, has expanded markedly since the 1990s, thanks mainly to the employment of skilled and even highly skilled staff. This is particularly evident in the field of health, where intermediate professions have grown very strongly. These changes inarguably increase the weight of the new middle class, particularly in the countries of the North and West whose economies depend on skilled services.

These processes have led to the emergence of a clearly defined group of countries where the middle class is numerous but the working class is much smaller than the European average (Map 2). These are mainly the countries which have succeeded in profiting from capitalist globalisation, and are located in the North and West of Europe, from the Scandinavian countries (Finland, Sweden, Denmark) to the English-speaking nations (United Kingdom, Ireland), and the countries of the West of the continent (the Netherlands, Germany, Belgium, Luxembourg, France).

*Map 2. The Middle Class in European Countries*

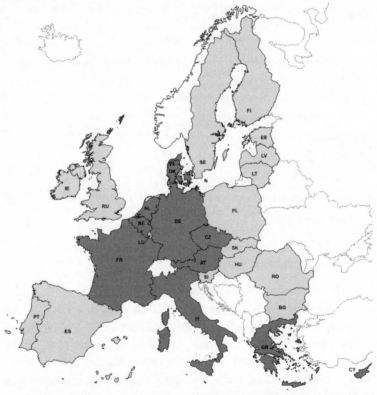

*Key*: Darker grey countries indicate a proportion of the middle class in work greater than the EU mean; lighter grey indicates a proportion lesser than the EU mean. On average the middle class represents 38 per cent of employed people, aged twenty-five to sixty-five, in Europe, EU 27 (excluding Malta). *Source*: LFS 2014.

Two subgroups can be distinguished here. In the Netherlands, Germany, Belgium and France, the middle-class and working-class populations are roughly equal in number. These are countries with high population density and a significant level of social protection which is linked to employment situation: individuals enjoy rights associated with the work they carry out.[4] The state remains a major provider of jobs, and the old middle class is still well established in the public sector. Germany, however, has recently seen a drastic reduction in unemployment benefit and a raising of the retirement age, substantially weakening the position of the German middle and working classes. In France these groups have been further destabilised by the deterioration in working conditions and increasing job insecurity. By contrast with these countries, the countries of the North (Finland, Sweden), the English-speaking countries (United Kingdom, Ireland) and Luxembourg have lower numbers of middle-class people than France and Germany and a relatively small working class.[5]

## The four subgroups of the middle class

Beyond these demographic and economic processes, we can identify four subgroups of the middle class in Europe. On the one hand, the middle class is divided vertically between public- and private-sector workers. On the other, this class is split between an 'upper' half, some of whose members share characteristics with the dominant class, and a 'lower' half, closer to the working class.

In the European Union, the contrast between the public-sector and the private-sector middle class is a long-standing phenomenon. Its historical significance varies across the continent, but everywhere it gives rise to considerable differences. Since there is

---

4   In Esping Andersen's terminology, this extensive social protection is characteristic of the conservative and corporatist regime of the countries of continental Europe. Gosta Esping Andersen, *The Three Worlds of Welfare Capitalism*, Cambridge: Polity Press, 1990.

5   It should be pointed out that Luxembourg is the only European country where the working class represents less than one-third of people of working age.

no standardised definition of public employment in Europe, these employees may be identified either by their sector of employment (administration, education, medical and social-welfare sectors) or by how they define themselves.[6] Irrespective of how they are defined, members of the middle class are characterised by a higher proportion of public-sector workers (between 30 and 40 per cent of those in work) than in the dominant class (between 20 and 30 per cent of those in work) or the European working class (a little over 10 per cent of those in work). Moreover, there are significantly more female workers in the middle-class public sector than in equivalent private-sector occupations. With the exception of law enforcement professions such as police officers and armed service personnel, women make up more than two-thirds of the middle class in the public sector. During the second half of the twentieth century, women benefited from the extension of state provision, particularly in Northern Europe.[7] However, even though they enjoy better pay and greater job stability than their counterparts in the private sector, middle-class women in the public sector have often found it difficult to achieve management positions.[8]

The divide between the public- and the private-sector middle class also reflects the different roles played by the state in different countries. In Belgium, Denmark, Sweden, France and the United Kingdom, between one-third and two-fifths of the middle-class population state that they work in the public sector. While their employment status may vary across countries, what unites these middle-class public-sector workers is that they provide services to the general public, in sectors relatively protected from international competition. In other European countries, the state plays a

6   In the EWCS 2015 survey, the question is posed thus: 'Do you work in [private sector; public sector; joint private-public sector; not-for-profit sector; other]?'

7   Jon Eivind Kolberg, 'The Gender Dimension of the Welfare State', *International Journal of Sociology* 21: 2, 1991, 119–48.

8   Wiji Arulampalam, Alison L. Boothe and Mark L. Bryan, 'Is There a Glass Ceiling over Europe? Exploring the Gender Pay Gap across the Wage Distribution', *Industrial and Labor Relations Review* 60: 2, 2007, 163–86.

less pronounced role and this has an impact both on job structure and on the composition of the middle class. In Eastern Europe, the transition to the market economy has resulted in privatisation and state downsizing taking place at varying rates, and on varying scales, depending on the country. In Bulgaria and the Czech Republic, for instance, the public sector employs barely one-third of the middle class.

A second split within the middle class pits an upper half, characterised by a certain degree of autonomy, against a lower half often found in positions of subordination. This divide is primarily related to educational inequalities, with occupations requiring higher qualifications in the upper half and those requiring less skill below. Less than a third of shopkeepers, office workers, receptionists, customer service clerks, police officers or members of the armed forces or security agents and owners of small hotels and restaurants have higher education qualifications, compared to approximately 40 per cent of science, engineering and ICT technicians; sales and administration associate professionals; and shop, hotel and restaurant managers; and nine out of ten teachers. The contrast between the most and the least highly qualified workers is also manifested in relative fear of unemployment: while teachers rarely experience this (fewer than 3 per cent), office workers, customer service clerks and receptionists are almost as likely to face unemployment as the working class (9 per cent).

Thus four subgroups of the middle class can be identified, depending on how they are positioned on either side of each of these divides. In the public sector, we have, on the one hand, teachers and associate professionals in the health, legal and social sectors who, thanks to their education and qualifications, make up the top half of the public-sector professions; on the other, non-commissioned officers, the police, armed service personnel, office workers and receptionists make up the bottom half. In the private sector, managers of shops, hotels and restaurants; science, engineering and ICT technicians; and sales and administration associate professionals are contrasted with security agents, office workers, receptionists, customer service clerks, shopkeepers, and, still more starkly, self-employed hotel and restaurant owners, who, given their low level of education, are closer to the working class.

*Table 7. Characteristics of the Socio-economic Groups Comprising the European Middle Class*

| | Women | Public and quasi-public sector | Higher education |
|---|---|---|---|
| Self-employed hotel and restaurant owners | 33 % | N/A | 26 % |
| Shop, hotel and restaurant managers | 43 % | N/A | 43 % |
| Teachers | 71 % | 96 % | 89 % |
| Science, engineering and ICT associate professionals | 17 % | 10 % | 37 % |
| Health associate professionals (e.g. nurses) | 80 % | 82 % | 33 % |
| Sales and administration associate professionals (e.g. accountants) | 59 % | 5 % | 43 % |
| Legal and social associate professionals | 67 % | 65 % | 47 % |
| Non-commissioned officers | 7 % | 98 % | 26 % |
| Shopkeepers | 47 % | N/A | 28 % |
| Office workers | 67 % | 23 % | 26 % |
| Receptionists and customer service clerks | 72 % | 20 % | 32 % |
| Police officers, armed service personnel and security agents | 14 % | 62 % | 20 % |
| Total middle class | 55 % | 39 % | 41 % |

*Source*: LFS 2014. *Population*: People in work aged between twenty-five and sixty-five, EU 27 (excluding Malta). Interpretation: among teachers, 71 per cent are women, 96 per cent work in the public or quasi-public sector and 89 per cent have higher education qualifications.

*Protected from unemployment but restricted by work constraints*
Unlike the working class, the European middle class appears relatively protected from the risk of unemployment. During the
economic crisis of 2011, only 5 per cent of middle-class people
aged over twenty-five experienced unemployment. This low
proportion is partly due to the substantial place of the public sector.
Of course, working directly or indirectly for the state, local authorities or public institutions does not provide the same job security
in every country. In France, for example, more than three-quarters
of these employees are civil servants, a status under which their
employment, salary, career advancement and retirement security
are guaranteed. In Germany, on the other hand, civil servants
represent only one-third of public employees, while in Sweden the
overwhelming majority of public-sector workers are subject to
regulations and conditions no different from those in the private
sector.[9] But, despite these national variations, public-sector
employees stay longer in their jobs and are less likely to be made
redundant. In 2011, the unemployment rate for members of the
middle class in the private sector was double that of those in the
public sector (6 per cent versus 3 per cent).

The state and state-related institutions offer a relative protection against unemployment for a substantial proportion of the
middle class, especially middle-class women, close to half of
whom work in the public sector.[10] In many countries, the managerial turn adopted by governments in office has consisted of
privatising sectors where manual workers were well established
(rail, post, energy) or reforming local administrations by downsizing and demanding improved productivity. As a result, the
collective campaigns initiated by the members of the middle class
revolve less around the fear of relocation and more around

---

9   Hugrée, Penissat and Spire, 'Differences between Public and
Private Sector Employees Following the Managerial Turn in European
States'.

10   Martina Dieckhoff, 'The Effect of Unemployment on Subsequent
Job Quality in Europe: A Comparative Study of Four Countries', *Acta
Sociologica* 54, 2011, 233–49.

attempts to improve their working conditions, their rights and their wages.

Members of this class also enjoy a relatively stable working environment compared to those in the working class, and this is reflected in more regular work schedules. More than two-thirds of the people in this group state that they work the same number of hours every week or the same days each week. These factors are crucial in the organisation of domestic life, especially for families with young children. Compared to the working class, the regular hours enjoyed by middle-class women make it easier for them to balance work and family lives. Most of these women are graduates, meaning that they are also much less likely to be unemployed. However, they are four times more likely to work part-time compared to men in the same class (28 per cent versus 7 per cent). This difference can partly be explained by the requirements of employers, but is also due to domestic constraints.

The European middle class, however, is forced to work to a timetable that imposes on employees the days worked. Having to work on Saturdays and Sundays is a prime example.

*Table 8. Weekend Work in Europe*

| 'In your main job, do you usually work . . .'? | Saturday | | Sunday | |
|---|---|---|---|---|
| | Men | Women | Men | Women |
| Dominant class | 17% | 15% | 9% | 9% |
| Middle class | 29% | 20% | 17% | 11% |
| Working class | 30% | 36% | 16% | 19% |

Source: LFS 2014. *Population*: People in work aged between twenty-five and sixty-five, EU 27 (excluding Malta).

The frequency of weekend working may be explained by the fact that the majority of the occupations performed by the middle class primarily involve contact with the public. Those in public-facing professions, such as nurses, armed service personnel and the police, as well as receptionists and customer service clerks, are the most likely to work at night and at weekends. Teachers and science, engineering and ICT technicians, in contrast, are rarely subject to the constraints of such work schedules.

Part-time work is also an important factor. The occupations where part-time working is least common are those in the upper half of the private-sector middle class, i.e. managers of shops, hotels or restaurants; science, engineering and ICT technicians; and sales and administration associate professionals. These, however, are also largely male-dominated professions.

There is a particularly marked contrast between middle-class employees in the public sector and self-employed middle-class workers in terms of weekly working hours. While between 7 and 12 per cent of health, legal and social associate professionals state that they work more than forty-one hours, almost three-quarters of those running small hotels, restaurants and shops are in this situation; they are predominantly male. On the one hand, we have women engaged in public-service jobs who work for shorter hours but are forced to work more unsocial hours, in a more constrained schedule. On the other hand, we have a greater proportion of men, either self-employed or employed in the private sector, who work significantly longer hours each week but are less likely to be obliged to work unsocial hours.

This divide has political repercussions. Middle-class public-sector employees, who often have greater cultural capital and are more attentive to the need to balance work and family life, are more likely to be attracted to left-wing parties, which are generally favourable to shorter working hours. However, self-employed members of the middle class or those in the private sector have greater financial capital and are more likely to attach greater value to work. They are thus more inclined to identify with the programmes of conservative parties which advocate easing 'constraints' on working hours.[11]

11   Oddbjorn Knutsen, 'The Impact of Sector Employment on Party Choice: A Comparative Study of Eight West European Countries', *European Journal of Political Research* 44: 4, 2005, 593–621.

*Contact with the public*

An additional feature of the middle class in Europe is that their jobs often involve contact with clients and/or the general public. More than half of middle-class people state that their job entails responding to a specific sector of the public all the time or most of the time. This proportion is well above that in the dominant class (+ 9 percentage points) and still higher than that in the working class (+ 15 percentage points). This distinctive feature is even more pronounced among women, especially those in the service sector where interaction is at the heart of the profession. It can be found in the public sector (teachers and health, legal and social associate professionals) but also among the middle class in the private sector, especially those working in retail who are regularly required to respond to customer requests. Up to 75 per cent of receptionists and customer service clerks, and of restaurant, hotel and small business owners, also regularly interact with the public. While these jobs appear to be relatively protected from performance-based assessments, they are also increasingly subject to client-based evaluation, which introduces a performance criterion that is just as stressful.

Members of the middle class in Europe are thus often employed in public-facing professions and are required to manage different types of requests on a daily basis. These may involve bureaucratic procedures, as is the case of customer service administrators, but also retail activities and taking care of sick people or those in difficulty. The relationship with users, clients or patients demands the so-called 'relational' and 'human' skills associated with these jobs, but these skills are not always certified by a qualification. While these interactions vary in nature, they are part of a special working arrangement and give rise to tensions on account of repetitive requests from the management – tensions that have been growing steadily since the mid-1990s.[12] Indeed, a significant proportion of employees' activities relies on the

---

12   Damien Merllié and Pascal Paoli, *Ten Years of Working Conditions in the European Union, Luxembourg*, Dublin: Office for Official Publications of the European Communities, Eurofound, 2001.

presentation of the self, on language and on self-monitoring. The difficulty lies in the need to respond to varied demands from clients or users who may be difficult to satisfy, especially in the local-authority and public-service sectors, where resources dwindle with each passing year. These public-facing professions require employees to represent their employer permanently and to work under the gaze of others. As a result, contradictory demands emerge, with the boss replaced by the motto 'the customer is always right', a process that began when market logic began to spread through many companies and administrations.[13] Regular and frequent contact with the public thus exposes these employees to stress, especially because the rhythm of work is determined by the number of requests and the immediate duties resulting from them. Since the 1990s,[14] work rhythms in Europe have increasingly been dictated by human demands or by colleagues' activities, and somewhat less by direct requests from superiors or automatic machine speeds.

In terms of working conditions, middle-class people in Europe are in a better position than those in the working class, since their occupations cut across several spheres. Within the middle class there are numerous structural contrasts: public/private, highly/poorly educated, protected from/at risk of unemployment, stable/unstable. These contrasts, taken together, make this group an artefact, which governments regularly attempt to present as a unified and tangible reality, to create the impression that they are addressing the whole of society.

---

13  Michel Gollac and Serge Volkoff, 'Citius, Altius, Fortius: L'intensification du travail', Actes de la recherche en sciences sociales 114, 1996, 54–67.

14  Brendan Burchell, Damien Cartron, Péter Csizmadia, Stanislas Delcampe, Michel Gollac, Miklós Illéssy, Edward Lorenz, Csaba Makó, Catherine O'Brien and Antoine Valeyre, Working Conditions in the European Union: Working Time and Work Intensity, Luxembourg: Office for Official Publications of the European Communities, 2009.

## MATERIAL COMFORT AND CULTURAL ASPIRATIONS

The middle class is also distinguished by its level of material comfort and cultural capital. For a long time, the middle class was characterised by its access to a variety of consumer goods (household appliances, computers, cars, leisure activities), access which now extends to all social classes and regions in Europe. In terms of property, however, housing remains a criterion distinguishing the middle class from the working class. While homeownership has also become widespread, the level of comfort in homes, and the amount of resources for acquiring property (debt-to-income ratio) create new social borders.

### The spread of a property-owning middle class

The considerable number of homeowners in Europe is in part a legacy of the twentieth century, during which access to property spread. Nevertheless, over Europe as a whole homeownership is a key component of inequality: behind the overall figure of 70 per cent of people who own property lie variations from country to country, and in type of housing. Acquiring one's own home often represents a necessary, though in itself insufficient, means of differentiating oneself from the working class. Nearly three-quarters of the middle class in Europe (72 per cent) own their homes, compared to two-thirds of the working class (66 per cent). Today, the middle class makes up almost half of all those who own their homes.

### Access to property in Europe

Homeownership has not spread at the same rate throughout Europe, being strongly influenced by the internal history of each country and by how the state has invested in the housing sector in the past. It is thus possible to distinguish three groups of countries, with three very different patterns of homeownership. In European countries where the state and local government play a major role, the level of homeownership is relatively low, albeit always over 50 per cent: 59 per cent in Austria, 64 per cent in France, 60 per cent in Denmark and 66 per cent in the Netherlands. In these countries, public housing for rent has long been of high quality, and it remains attractive to the working class as well as to a large proportion of the middle class. Germany, with only 50 per cent private homeowners, stands out here: housing policy in the wake of the Second World War involved intervention in the public and private housing market in an attempt to ensure good-quality housing was available at very low rents. Following the reunification of Germany, financial support for buying a home was revived during the 1990s, but Germany still has one of the lowest rates of homeownership in Europe.

In this first group of countries, the number of homeowners has been increasing from year to year, as the state withdraws from the sector and public policy supporting homeownership through low-cost loans becomes widespread.[15] At the same time, however, property prices have been rising, leading to a generational divide between those who already own their homes and younger people, for whom the cost of homeownership is growing, making it more and more difficult for them to enter the private housing market.

The proportion of homeowners is slightly higher in the South of Europe (70 per cent in Italy, 76 per cent in Portugal, and 76 per cent in Spain), where rental property has long been very limited. Access to property is very often made possible by financial assistance from the extended family, a support that has been used to offset the shortcomings of the social-welfare system.[16] Without a guaranteed pension, owning a home, even with a mortgage, represents a means to secure the future. Lastly, in the countries of the former Eastern Bloc, the dismantling of communist regimes has been accompanied by a widespread rise in property ownership: 83 per cent in Poland, 91 per cent in Slovakia and 96 per cent in Romania. In Romania, the majority of public housing was sold to the occupants during the collapse of communism or shortly

---

15  Mary Ann Stamsø, 'Housing and Welfare Policy: Changing Relations? A Cross-national Comparison', *Housing, Theory and Society* 27: 1, 2010, 64–75.

16  Chris Allen, *Housing Market Renewal and Social Class Formation*, London: Routledge, 2008.

thereafter. The few people still renting are mainly Roma, who are excluded from homeownership and subjected to evictions without rehousing, under a policy that seeks to ensure the restitution of property nationalised under the communist regime to its original owners or their descendants.

While homeownership is closely linked to country of residence, it remains, nevertheless, a distinctive feature of the middle class across Europe, acting both as a buffer against vagaries of the economic situation and as a resource that makes it possible to plan for the future.

That said, not all middle-class households have access to property. The probability of owning one's home is highly dependent on employment status: self-employed people are more likely to own their homes than employees (77 versus 68 per cent); middle-class public-sector workers are more likely to own their home than their counterparts in the private sector (72 versus 69 per cent). Job security is not only a resource that allows people to overcome the restrictions associated with mortgage loans[17] – it also makes it possible to plan for the future.

The divide is also age-related: 57 per cent of the middle class aged between twenty-five and thirty-four are homeowners, compared to 79 per cent among the over-fifty-fives. This gap results from two factors. First, couples at the start of their working lives have fewer savings than those close to retirement. On top of this comes the generational factor. The financial crisis of 2008 and its consequences in Europe led to a reduction in the proportion of new buyers by primarily penalising those who had no inheritance from their parents.[18]

The costs incurred differ depending on whether the home is bought outright or with a mortgage. Here again, employment

---

17   Philipp M. Lersch and Carolin Dewilde, 'Employment Insecurity and First-Time Homeownership: Evidence from Twenty-Two European Countries', *Environment and Planning A* 47: 3, 2015, 607–25.

18   Karin Kurz and Hans-Peter Blossfeld (eds.), *Home Ownership and Social Inequality in a Comparative Perspective*, Stanford: Stanford University Press, 2004.

status reveals small differences within the middle class. Among middle-class employees who own their home, 53 per cent are paying a mortgage, while only 40 per cent of their self-employed counterparts are in this position. But it is non-nationals who stand out the most. Three-quarters of Europeans who are citizens of their country of residence own their homes; the same is true for less than half of non-EU citizens. For households with mortgages, interest rates vary greatly depending on the ability to negotiate with banks and obtain financial aid from families. The cost of homeownership thus no longer depends on macroeconomic indicators but rather on individual social and financial resources.

In order to go beyond the simplistic account of a middle class in which the vast majority own their homes, quality of housing must also be taken into account. Recent decades have seen a significant improvement in the quality of housing and, at the same time, an increasingly rapid rise in property prices. In a Europe in which the availability of rental properties varies widely from one country to another, patterns of homeownership can be distinguished on the basis of a number of comfort criteria. The number of rooms, in relation to size of household, is a key feature. Housing can thus be differentiated depending on whether the number of rooms is higher (spacious) or lower (overcrowded) than the number of people living there. According to this distinction, 69 per cent of middle-class homeowners have spacious housing, compared to 56 per cent in the working class and 74 per cent in the dominant class.

Other elements of comfort can also be taken into account, such as street noise, local crime rates, and material aspects such as light levels, a private shower or bath, an indoor toilet or a roof in good condition. Combining all these criteria reveals that more than half (53 per cent) of middle-class homeowners state that they have at least one problem with the comfort of their homes. This proportion is significantly higher among working-class homeowners in Europe (64 per cent). Middle-class homeowners in rural areas experience these problems less (45 per cent) than those in urban areas (58 per cent).

There are also significant variations between the three groups of countries distinguished above. In Western and Northern Europe, more than half of middle-class homeowners own homes that meet all comfort criteria: 59 per cent in the United Kingdom, 56 per cent in France, and 70 per cent in Finland. In Mediterranean countries, roughly half as many middle-class homeowners enjoy the same comfort: 24 per cent in Greece, 29 per cent in Italy and 39 per cent in Portugal. On the outskirts of these countries' major cities, there is still a substantial stock of housing that lacks even basic facilities such as running water and electricity. Dilapidated dwellings can also be found both within city centres and in rural areas. In the absence of state intervention, property in the private housing sector comes at a high cost for a relatively low level of comfort.[19] Lastly, in Central and Eastern Europe, homeowners constitute the overwhelming majority of the middle class, but very few of their houses fulfil all the comfort criteria: 19 per cent in Bulgaria, 29 per cent in Slovakia and 29 per cent in Poland. Romania is undoubtedly the most extreme case: here 97 per cent of the middle class own their homes, but only 10 per cent say they have the main comfort criteria.

Thus the majority of middle-class people in the EU own their homes, but this is far from a unifying, homogenising factor: the meaning of ownership varies according to the country concerned, employment status and area of residence. Debt and comfort levels suggest that internal hierarchies exist among homeowners.

### Cultural capital that brings the middle class closer to the dominant class

The proximity of the middle class to the dominant class is clearly reflected in cultural practices. Here again, however, the internal divisions are so marked that it is difficult to identify

---

19   Alfredo Bruto da Costa, Ana Cardoso, Isabel Baptista and Pedro Perista, 'The Dynamics of Income Poverty and Social Exclusion in Portugal', in Eleni Apospori and Jane Millar (eds.), *The Dynamics of Social Exclusion in Europe: Comparing Austria, Germany, Greece, Portugal and the UK*, Northampton: Edward Elgar, 2003.

them as a homogeneous group. Where cultural practices are concerned, the parents' level of education is a primary indicator of cultural capital, which refers to a set of cultural attitudes and practices.

Among the middle class in Europe, 54 per cent of people have fathers who did not complete high school, compared to only 39 per cent of the dominant class. However, there are considerable variations depending on the subgroup to which the individual belongs. First, middle-class people working in the public sector are more often likely to have inherited a cultural capital from their father than those in the private sector. Second, teachers, 25 per cent of whom have a father with higher education, are distinguished from small business owners in the hospitality and retail sectors, retailers, office workers, police officers, soldiers and security personnel, of whom fewer than one in ten are in the same situation. The inequalities between the public and private sectors and between the upper and lower sections of the middle class are the same with regard to the mother's level of education.

The contrast within the middle class between those with the greatest financial capital – private-sector employees and the self-employed – and those with greater cultural capital – such as teachers – marks a distinction between two different ways of rising up the social scale. Reading practices clearly reveal this (see Table 9). Reading books is an activity which brings the middle class in Europe closer to the dominant class, and clearly distinguishes them from the working class. There is, however, a contrast between those working in the public sector, who are more likely to be readers, and their counterparts in the private sector (84 versus 70 per cent). This divide is, of course, reinforced by the impact of education: legal, health and social associate professionals, and especially teachers, clearly stand out from lower-middle-class people such as police officers, armed service personnel, security agents, and owners of small businesses in the hospitality and retail sectors, but also, to a lesser degree, from middle-class people working in the private sector (shop, hotel and restaurant managers; science, engineering and ICT technicians; and sales and administration associate professionals).

*Table 9. Reading Practices in Europe*

| 'Over the last twelve months, have you read a book during your free time?' | | Yes | No |
|---|---|---|---|
| Middle class | Self-employed hotel and restaurant owners | 53% | 47% |
| | Shop, hotel and restaurants managers | 69% | 31% |
| | Teachers | 91% | 9% |
| | Science, engineering and ICT associate professionals | 71% | 29% |
| | Health associate professionals (e.g. nurses) | 84% | 16% |
| | Business and administration associate professionals | 81% | 19% |
| | Legal and social associate professionals | 84% | 16% |
| | Non-commissioned officers | N/A | N/A |
| | Shopkeepers | 65% | 35% |
| | Office workers | 73% | 27% |
| | Receptionists and customer service clerks | 78% | 22% |
| | Police officers, armed service personnel and security agents | 56% | 44% |
| Dominant class | | 84% | 16% |
| Middle class | | 76% | 24% |
| Working class | | 56% | 43% |

*Source*: AES 2011. *Population*: EU 27 (excluding Denmark, Ireland, Belgium, United Kingdom, France, the Netherlands, Sweden, Malta), people in work aged between twenty-five and sixty-five. Interpretation: 76 per cent of middle-class people in work have read a book in the last twelve months as part of their leisure activities.

Variations in reading practices thus reinforce the hypothesis of four subgroups within the middle class in Europe. Investment in the mastery of information and communications technology skills is also a significant distinguishing criterion. Individuals with ICT skills are at a significant advantage when applying for any job that involves working digitally.[20]

The cultural capital accumulated by a section of the middle class may even be converted into political power under certain circumstances. For instance, between the 1960s and the 1980s, teachers throughout Europe became parliamentary representatives, sometimes taking up nearly one-fifth of parliamentary seats.[21] Although this figure has fallen slightly since the 1990s, it remains a sign of teachers' involvement in public affairs.

Nevertheless, it appears that the middle class's advantage in terms of cultural capital is no longer sufficient to guarantee upward social mobility. In many countries, more widespread access to higher education has resulted in new forms of selection based more on the possession of financial capital. In the United Kingdom, students from middle-class families are well aware that qualifications alone no longer guarantee an upward trajectory, as they did for their parents. They must be able to draw on financial resources, their parents' social networks and, more broadly, networks built throughout their studies and careers.[22] In Germany, an increasing number of young university graduates are no longer able to find a job quickly.[23] Faced with conditions of insecurity, only substantial financial capital can help them sustain themselves in this situation of uncertainty. The social-mobility model based on cultural meritocracy is thus in crisis, raising the question of what political role the middle class in Europe will be able to play in the future.

20 Daron Acemoglu, 'Technical Change, Inequality, and the Labor Market', *Journal of Economic Literature* 40: 1, 2002, 7–72.

21 Maurizio Cotta, Pedro Tavares de Almeida and Christophe Le Roux, 'De serviteurs de l'Etat à représentants élus: Les parlementaires originaires du secteur public en Europe', *Pôle sud* 21, 2004, 101–22.

22 Ann Mary Bathmaker, Nicola Ingram and Richard Waller, 'Higher Education, Social Class and the Mobilisation of Capitals: Recognising and Playing the Game', *British Journal of Sociology of Education* 34: 5–6, 2013, 723–43.

23 Franz Schultheis and Kristina Schulz (eds), *Gesellschaft mit begrenzter Haftung: Zumutungen und Leiden im deutschen Alltag*, UVK Verlagsgesellschaft mbH, Konstanz, 2005.

## THE PARADOXES OF THE POLITICAL ROLE OF THE MIDDLE CLASS

The relative heterogeneity of the middle class across Europe gives it a paradoxical political status. Unlike the working class, it is difficult to identify what its members have in common, despite the fact that the majority of Europeans identify themselves as 'middle-class'. However, the shared sense of belonging to this group is becoming predominant at a time when some argue that it may be on the way to disappearing.

### Expansion or disappearance of the middle class?

In Northern and Western Europe, the people who identify as middle-class far exceed the objective borders of this social group (see Appendix 3). Several historical trends help explain this alignment. First, the loss of a sense of belonging to the working class left a void which was largely filled by much more consensual discourses that trumpeted the stability of the middle class. In addition, the rise of social-welfare systems was accompanied by a promise of upward mobility that presents the middle class as synonymous with material comfort and personal fulfilment. Lastly, the important role played by redistribution systems also helped enhance the status of this social group by presenting it as the symbol of the reduction of inequality.

But these trends have manifested in different ways across Europe. In the Scandinavian countries, for example, there is a strong sense of belonging to an egalitarian middle-class society. Responses to the question of countries' social structure fall into two camps. On the one hand, the image of a society 'in which most people are in the middle' is favoured by Norwegians and Swedes. On the other, the majority of French people and a large proportion of Germans feel they belong to a pyramidal society.[24] In other European countries, the sense of belonging to the middle class is

---

24   Johs Hjellbrekke, Vegard Jarness and Olav Korsnes, 'Cultural Distinctions in an "Egalitarian" Society', in Philippe Coulangeon and Julien Duval (eds), *The Routledge Companion to Bourdieu's Distinction*, London: Routledge, 2014, 187–206, 189.

also shared by the majority; this is a result of somewhat different social processes.

For a long time, the great majority in the former communist countries identified themselves as belonging to the working class. This class was the most highly regarded, mainly because of the aura conferred on it by state institutions. The trend was reversed after 1989, and the collapse of the USSR and its allies. In Bulgaria, Hungary and Poland, the term 'middle class' became increasingly associated with the stabilisation of social order.[25] This was also the case in the Czech Republic, where the extolling of the middle class became, over the years, a media cliché that helped maintain a promise of prosperity while ignoring the discourse on social inequalities.[26] A powerful fascination with the middle class thus became established in several countries in this region, and this went hand in hand with an almost simultaneous decline in analysis in terms of social class. By the late 2000s, most people thus identified themselves as belonging to the middle class. In Poland, for instance, while almost 40 per cent of adults identified as working-class in the 2000s, this figure had fallen to only one-third in the 2010s, compared to the 50 per cent who identified as middle-class.[27] Overall, the term 'middle class' has remained synonymous with economic stability and upward mobility in the collective psyche throughout Europe, despite the fact that the effects of the 2008 crisis have weakened this social group, the outlines of which vary from one country to another.

Notwithstanding predictions of the disappearance of the middle class,[28] automation and the so-called 'digital economy' pose the

25    David Ost, 'Stuck in the Past and the Future: Class Analysis in Postcommunist Poland', *East European Politics and Societies* 29: 3, 2015, 610–24.

26    Jan Drahokoupil, 'Class in Czechia: The Legacy of Stratification Research', *East European Politics and Societies* 29: 3, 2015, 577–87.

27    Statistics from the World Values Survey: 1995–9, 2005–9, 2010–14.

28    Randall Collins, 'The End of Middle-Class Work: No More Escapes', in Immanuel Wallerstein, Randall Collins, Michael Mann, Georgi Derluguian and Craig Calhoun, *Does Capitalism Have a Future?*, New York: Oxford University Press, 2013, 37–69.

greatest threat to the working class, either by eliminating specific professions in the industrial sector or by reducing job security. In all other professions, there is still a high proportion of middle-class people, but they are in a weaker position than executives, mainly because their skills are less adaptable to changes in the labour market. The common feature of these workers now thus appears to be the fear of being downgraded, rather than the increasingly tenuous hope that they will one day be able to join the European elite. Yet this anxiety, which has been widely exploited politically in many countries in Europe, does not mean that they are actually moving down in society. The position of the middle class on the labour market, and its members' access to consumer goods, remain considerably stronger than those of the working class. Rather, what they are experiencing is lower earning prospects and reduced social mobility compared to previous generations in the same social group.

### Uneven levels of political mobilisation among the middle class

The 2008 crisis affected the middle class throughout Europe. On the one hand, young graduates found their future prospects blighted, while on the other, middle-class people working in the public sector experienced a sharp deterioration in their working conditions following drastic cuts in state budgets. However, reactions have varied widely across countries.

In countries of Northern and Western Europe, the deterioration in job prospects has resulted in a generational divide between the older members of the middle class, who enjoyed a degree of upward mobility in the 1980s, and younger people, who entered the labour market in the 2000s, and whose future appears much less secure. This generational divide is apparent particularly in income distribution and working conditions, but has not led everywhere to political expressions of dissatisfaction. Ireland, for example, responded to the 2008 economic crisis with an increase in progressive household taxes and drastic cuts in public spending, giving rise to the popular expression 'squeezed middle'.[29] But this

29   Brian Nolan, Christopher T. Whelan, Emma Calvert, Tony Fahey, Deirdre Healy, Aogan Mulcahy, Bertrand Maître and Michelle Norris,

did not result in any great political mobilisation, except occasionally during elections when candidates campaigning to leave the EU received more votes.

This trend was more evident in Finland, where the True Finns party made a historic breakthrough in the 2011 elections. This victory has been firmly associated with the middle class. The True Finns party, which supports redistributive policies, is more left-wing in terms of economic policy but leans towards conservatism on social issues, in its hostility towards immigration, and in its trenchant opposition to the EU.[30] In the United Kingdom, those who voted for Brexit were generally members of the middle and working classes affected by deindustrialisation, often living far from the major cities. In the South and East of Europe, on the other hand, where the middle class was destabilised on three levels (by growing unemployment, the segmentation of the labour market and rising taxes), there were a number of protests in Portugal, Spain and Greece. These protests shared several common features: they were led by the younger generation of graduates, and they were organised relatively spontaneously through networks, predominantly online.

In Portugal, the middle-class reaction to the austerity policies required by the country's creditors (the IMF and the ECB) took two forms: mobilisation and flight. At the height of the crisis, in 2012, 10,000 Portuguese were leaving the country each month, a figure higher than that in the 1960s. The difference, however, was that, rather than agricultural workers and tradespeople, it was engineers and scientists who were now leaving, and that they viewed not France but Brazil as the land of opportunity. At the same time, the country was hit by repeated conflicts: between 2010

---

'Ireland: Inequality and Its Impact in Boom and Bust', in Brian Nolan, Wiemer Salverda, Daniele Checci, Ive Marx, Abbigail McKnight, Istvan Giörgy Toth and Herman van de Werfhorst, *Changing Inequalities and Societal Impact in Rich Countries*, Oxford: Oxford University Press, 2014, 354.

30   Jenni Blomgren, Heikki Hiilamo, Olli Kangas and Mikko Niemelä, 'Finland: Growing Inequality with Contested Consequences', in Nolan et al., *Changing Inequalities*, 241.

and 2012, there were 384 strikes, involving 224,500 workers, in the private sector alone.[31] Trade unions quickly lost their monopoly on organising protest, and campaigns extended well beyond the confines of the workplace. On 12 March 2011, between 300,000 and 400,000 people took part in demonstrations called by the group Geração à Rasca ('Broke Generation'). Young people have been at the forefront of these movements, for good reason: between 2011 and 2012, unemployment in the fifteen–twenty-four age group rose from 27 per cent to 36 per cent, double the national average. More broadly, these movements reflect the disillusionment of middle-class Portuguese public-sector workers: teachers, nurses and other hospital workers have been the driving force behind these protests at a time when the working class appears to have lost its fighting spirit.

Spain has also experienced large-scale demonstrations manifesting fury at the state's failure to protect its citizens and to guarantee a decent standard of living. The collapse of the housing bubble ruined many households that had qualified for mortgages prior to the crisis and some people were even evicted from their homes. At the same time, unemployment rose to nearly 25 per cent of the workforce, with young graduates being particularly hard hit, and some being forced into exile. This economic and social crisis found its political response in the Indignados movement, which, following mass demonstrations in the spring of 2011, received strong popular support. As a result, Podemos, a party that brings together middle- and working-class people, many of them young city dwellers, made an electoral breakthrough. In Greece, the financial crisis and exasperation at the collusion of the political and economic elites brought Syriza to power, with the promise of sweeping reforms. Unlike Podemos, Alexis Tsipras's party was able to expand its appeal to older voters and especially to members of the middle class in the private sector and to farmers. In contrast, protests have been less vehement in the countries of Central and

---

31  Elisio Estanque, 'Middle-Class Rebellions? Precarious Employment and Social Movements in Portugal and Brazil (2011–2013)', *RCCS Annual Review* 7, 2015, 17–44.

Eastern Europe than in Southern Europe, and discontent brought nationalist governments to power. Viktor Orbán's accession to power in Hungary in 2010 announced the emergence of a conservative movement vehemently opposed to political liberalism, and this then spread elsewhere. In Poland, the ultraconservatives in the Law and Justice Party also took advantage of the middle and working class's anxieties about the European project, thus winning the 2015 elections with a vote that reached around 85 per cent in rural areas. In 2016, Bulgaria elected a Russia-oriented president whose campaign had been openly hostile to the European Union. In Romania and Slovakia, social-democratic parties won parliamentary elections thanks to a programme that rejected immigration and fell in line with the demands of the far right.

Across the different regions of Europe, members of the middle class thus responded in different ways to the deterioration of their position on the labour market. However, they have continued to play a decisive role in social and political changes.

At both European and national levels, the middle class operates as a unifying symbol, despite the fact that it can be difficult to describe as homogeneous. In terms of both working conditions and standards of living, the middle class in Europe is riven with internal divisions related to employment status and the gendered structure of professions, and still more to whether they work in the public or the private sector. However, the neoliberal reforms of the last thirty years have influenced these divides in different ways. On the one hand, the challenge to the status of public-sector employees has brought their working conditions closer to those in the private sector. On the other, the fact that some differences remain – for example in terms of qualification levels and job security – is increasingly masked by a unifying discourse that denigrates those living on welfare benefits and extols work and the deserving middle class.

In many countries, the middle class remains a focus of identification, and even a rallying point for those who feel they have suffered most from the crisis. Paradoxically, while they appear relatively safe compared to the working class across Europe, some sections of the middle class are nevertheless much more active in defending their interests, both in elections and sometimes in demonstrations. Thus it is middle-class public-sector employees who have campaigned most vociferously against austerity policies, despite the fact that they have been relatively sheltered from the effects of globalisation compared to other groups. However, while this class played a pivotal role in the development of nation states, it is unclear whether it will play a comparable part in the future, given that many of its members are yet to perceive the European project as synonymous with social emancipation.

# 3

# Beyond the 1 Per Cent: The Plural Domination of the European Dominant Class

## DEFINING THE DOMINANT CLASS

The elite is often perceived as a class of exploiters and predators of wealth, who possess more resources than the rest of the world's population put together, a fact regularly condemned by the major NGOs or the Occupy Wall Street movement, which denounces the yawning gap between the 99 per cent (the people) and the 1 per cent (the super-rich). However, these super-rich need allies to ensure that their orders at work will be transmitted and fulfilled, and ultimately to secure their hegemonic position in society.

Isolating the tiny topmost tip of the social pyramid would mean overlooking the role of other sections of the globally privileged group. To describe those who share a common relation to the rules, we decided to use the term 'dominant class'. Following Mills's definition,[1] it is an 'alliance' that encompasses several 'institutional orders' which are spatially and historically independent but which are linked to the interests of this globally privileged group. Social order is maintained and reproduced largely because the dominant class is organised in concentric circles, in terms of either financial or cultural capital. Our analysis in terms of patterns of dominance has therefore led us to retain a broad definition of the dominant

---

1   Charles Wright Mills, *The Power Elite*, New York: Oxford University Press, 1958.

class, within which distinctions may be drawn between those who have power in the economic sphere (owners of large enterprises and managing directors), those who have power in the state apparatus (high-ranking civil servants) and those who are able to impose their prescriptions on the basis of their depth of expert knowledge (doctors, lawyers and those in intellectual and cultural professions). This approach allows us to emphasise processes of social appropriation of resources that are not restricted to income but also include cultural and symbolic capital. This accumulation of several forms of capital forms the basis for their dominant position in every European country. It draws attention not only to the fact that their dominance is rooted in the economic market but also to a work of legitimisation that extends to every aspect of daily life: living in privileged places, determining the working conditions of other employees, achieving high-level qualifications, engaging intensively in leisure practices and, lastly, being able to speak English.

The lifestyles and cultural affinities of members of the dominant class make this a homogeneous group, despite internal divisions and contradictions. European statistical surveys often focus on poverty or unemployment and thus provide few indicators enabling us to measure the mechanisms of dominance. We therefore propose to draw on an amalgamated set of indices, in order to sketch the outline of the dominant class at the European level.

## THE ECONOMIC ASCENDANCY OF THE DOMINANT CLASS

Predominantly male, the employed members of the dominant class form a relatively large social group comprising nearly 20 per cent of Europeans. Their power is primarily economic, drawn from the forms of subordination they impose in the world of work, and on their financial resources.

### The three subgroups of the dominant class

The dominant class in Europe as we have defined it can be broken down into three subgroups. The first of these (20 per cent of the dominant class in Europe) consists of those who occupy managerial positions in companies and public bodies. Commonly referred to as 'managers' in English-speaking countries, we will refer to them here as senior managers. In both the public and the private sectors, these are the people who earn the highest incomes; the primary role of 90 per cent of them is to supervise the work of other employees. The members of this group are also relatively older than the average for the dominant class, are more likely to be male (31 per cent women compared to an average of 41 per cent for the dominant class as a whole), and are long-established in their senior positions.

The second subgroup comprises those with high-level academic qualifications and specialist knowledge in their field. This pole brings together intellectual and scientific professions: engineers and specialists in science, engineering and information technology (25 per cent of the group); managers in administration, finance and business (20 per cent);[2] doctors and other health specialists (15 per cent); lawyers, judges, journalists and artists (15 per cent). With the exception of engineers, women predominate in this subgroup: 70 per cent of doctors and other health specialists; 56 per cent of lawyers, judges, journalists and artists; and almost 50 per cent of administration, finance and business managers are women. They are also younger, better educated and more professionally mobile than the average for the dominant class. Moreover, while doctors, other health specialists and judges work primarily in the public sector, the majority of the other intellectual professions fall in the private sector. This difference has some consequences for working conditions.

Finally, the third subgroup consists of chief executive officers (5 per cent) – entrepreneurs[3] – and may be described as the lowest

2    Administration, finance and business managers differ from senior managers in that they specialise in particular types of work thanks to their specific skills or knowledge. Moreover, these managers are usually placed under the direction of senior managers in organisational charts. Senior managers are called on to represent companies or organisations, establish key goals and orientations, set budgets, and monitor and evaluate the performance of one or more departments.

3    This group has greater financial and cultural capital than small business owners in the hotel, catering and retail sector (self-employed hotel and restaurant owners), whom we have included in the middle class.

tier of the dominant class. Older, predominantly male (only one in five is female) and longer-established in their post than those in senior intellectual professions, members of this subgroup have a considerably lower level of qualifications (– 30 percentage points), but enjoy very comfortable standards of living despite earning less than the members of the other two subgroups.

*Table 10. Socio-economic Groups within the Dominant Class in Europe*

| | |
|---|---|
| Senior managers | 20% |
| Engineers, scientists and ICT professionals | 25% |
| Doctors and other healthcare specialists | 15% |
| Managers in administration, finance and business | 20% |
| Lawyers, judges, journalists and artists | 15% |
| Chief executive officers | 5% |
| Total dominant class | 100% |

*Source*: LFS 2014. *Population*: People in work aged between twenty-five and sixty-five, EU 27 (excluding Malta).

### Privileged locations

In the North and West of Europe, the dominant class is larger than in other countries, representing around a quarter of those in work, much higher than the European average of 19 per cent (Map 3).

In these countries, the disproportionate size of the dominant class is due partly to the major significance of the financial sector and highly skilled services. On the one hand, Finland and Sweden, which have the highest levels of private investment in research and development, have specialised in the export of highly innovative products: in the 1990s and 2000s, Nokia, the mobile-phone manufacturer, was a driving force in the Finnish economy, to the extent that it represented up to 4 per cent of the country's GDP. In Sweden exports have been spearheaded for the last several years by environmental technology. The wealth accrued from these advantages has been more or less shared throughout the population, through

*Map 3. The Dominant Class in European Countries*

*Key:* Darker grey countries indicate a proportion of the dominant class in work greater than the EU mean; lighter grey indicates a proportion lesser than the EU mean. On average the dominant class represents 19 per cent of employed people, aged twenty-five to sixty-five, in Europe, EU 27 (excluding Malta). *Source:* LFS 2014.

a highly redistributive system that mitigates inequalities.[4] On the other hand, the strategies of the English-speaking nations and Luxembourg have centred primarily on a fiscal policy highly favourable to the foreign companies that have set up there, offering

---

4   Joh Kvist, Johan Fritzell, Bjorn Hvinden and Olli Kangas (eds), *Changing Social Equality: The Nordic Welfare Model in the Twenty-First Century*, Bristol and Chicago: Policy Press, 2012.

multinationals access to the European market. The dominant class in Britain, Luxembourg and Ireland has profited substantially from these extra-European investments, but other working people in these countries have seen very little benefit. Evidently, the predominance of the dominant and middle classes that is typical of a number of European countries conceals configurations of class that differ from one nation to another. The situation is very different in Central and Eastern Europe, where the dominant class represents only a small minority – a fact that can be explained by the control, one might even say stranglehold, that some Western firms hold over entire sectors of the economy. The region shares this latter characteristic with countries such as Greece, particularly since the 2008 crisis. They now also have in common a limited state presence and a fiscal and social system that does little to redistribute wealth. Within this group of countries, however, the Baltic states stand out for their larger dominant class, bringing them a little closer to the countries of Northern and Western Europe.

While members of the dominant class are over-represented in the North and West of Europe, more than half of them live in cities (54 per cent compared to 34 per cent of the working class). This distribution represents a historical reversal that is underlined in Savage's reading of Piketty's work:[5] the 'upper class' now earns its income from urban infrastructure, rather than from the agricultural land that used to provide its revenue. As a result, they also increasingly live in urban areas. Nowadays, in many cities, the dominant class has come together in order to preserve a space for its own community. In the largest European cities, the replacement of the working class by the middle and dominant classes – gentrification – has been under way for some time, and is manifested in the relegation of the working class to the fringes of urban zones. In London, urban renewal began in the 1980s, under Margaret Thatcher, with the expansion of business premises and luxury housing, particularly around the City. The neighbourhoods that had fallen prey to urban decay following the departure of industrial enterprises (mainly in

---

5   Mike Savage, 'Piketty's Challenge for Sociology', *British Journal of Sociology* 65: 4, 2014, 591–606.

the furniture and clothing industries) were taken over by art galleries, luxury boutiques and hip bars. Subsequently, under Tony Blair's 'Urban Renaissance' programme, which aimed to encourage the middle class to return to city centres, entertainment and the creative professions replaced industrial workers. In Amsterdam, social housing for a long time constituted the majority of residential property, but in recent years the municipal authorities have also promoted an urban regeneration policy that, under the guise of social diversity, supports acquisition of property by members of the middle class, who now live in the old workers' districts that have been completely transformed by gentrification.[6]

Similar processes of gentrification of capitals, although more recent, can also be seen in the countries of Central and Eastern Europe, in Prague and Budapest; this is linked to the identification of city centres as national heritage sites, and to their new focus on tourism. At the same time, spaces reserved for the dominant class (sometimes including gated communities, to which access is strictly controlled) have been developed close to the business districts: Docklands in London, Levallois in Paris, Milano Due in Milan.[7] In the European metropolises, segregation is first and foremost the privilege of the rich, particularly executives in the private sector.[8]

### The power to determine working conditions
The different subgroups in the top rung of society share a number of common features that are clearly visible in the world of work. The first characteristic of members of the dominant class in Europe is the autonomy granted them, or rather the autonomy they accord themselves, at work. The vast majority of the dominant class may

---

6    Wouter van Gent, 'Neoliberalization, Housing Institutions and Variegated Gentrification: How the "Third Wave" Broke in Amsterdam', *International Journal of Urban and Regional Research* 37: 2, 2013, 503–22.

7    Bruno Cousin, 'Classes supérieures de promotion et entre-soi résidentiel: L'agrégation affinitaire dans les quartiers refondés de Milan', *Espaces et sociétés* 150, 2012, 85–105.

8    Ray Forrest, Sin Yee Koh and Bart Wissink (eds), *Cities and the Super-Rich: Real Estate, Elite Practices and Urban Political Economies*, Basingstoke: Palgrave Macmillan, 2017.

take breaks at their workplace whenever they like – a proportion much higher than that in the middle class (+ 16 percentage points) and the working class (+ 26 percentage points). They are also much more likely than the other social groups to state that they can easily take an hour or two off work to deal with personal or family issues (+ 10 percentage points compared to the middle class and + 15 percentage points compared to the working class).

But this autonomy goes well beyond their ability to control their work rhythms, extending to the overall organisation of their work, their goals and what their roles entail. Moreover, members of the dominant class tend to occupy supervisory and managerial positions that enable them to influence the working conditions of other employees. Most of them are instrumental in changes that transform employees' working arrangements (64 per cent) and they are often consulted before being assigned new goals (62 per cent). This proximity to the organisational power of corporations is most apparent among senior managers and engineers. These characteristics point to a fundamental feature of the dominant class: an instrumental relationship with regulation whereby it represents for them not an externally imposed constraint but a variable they can always act upon.

The power they wield over the other classes in terms of working arrangements goes hand in hand with their certainty of career advancement. While 37 per cent of EU citizens consider that their work offers good prospects for career progression, this figure rises to 55 per cent among members of the dominant class. Senior managers, engineers and administrative, financial and business managers are those most confident in their chances of such progression. Chief executive officers in this group are more confident about their potential professional progression than self-employed hotel and restaurant owners (whom we have categorised as middle-class).

Finally, since the 1980s, the increase in exemptions from or reductions in taxes and social-security contributions, aimed at developing the personal-services industry, has led to the resurgence of a culture of domesticity, much to the advantage of the dominant class. Beauty care, ICT support, gardening and domestic services all improve day-to-day comfort, and are subject to tax incentives in many countries. Power relations are not restricted to the workplace, but are also reproduced in the private sphere through the accumulation of domestic employees.

## The art of accumulating financial wealth

The professional flexibility the dominant class enjoys derives from its income, predominantly that from work, which assures it material comfort and bright prospects, in contrast to the working class, where uncertainty about the future and hence dependency on relatives or the state continue to predominate. Indeed, members of the dominant class are distinguished primarily by their financial wealth, which can be measured by the revenues declared in European statistical surveys (Table 11).

*Table 11. Incomes in the EU*

|  | Median gross annual income | Median total gross household income | Median equivalised household disposable income |
|---|---|---|---|
| Chief executive officers | N/A | 48,500 | 19,200 |
| Senior managers | 42,100 | 72,300 | 29,300 |
| Engineers and specialists in science, engineering and information technology | 37,100 | 61,300 | 25,300 |
| Doctors and other healthcare specialists | 28,500 | 62,300 | 25,700 |
| Administration, finance and business managers | 32,200 | 59,100 | 25,600 |
| Lawyers, judges, journalists and artists | 26,000 | 49,600 | 22,900 |
| **Total dominant class** | **34,400** | **63,700** | **25,800** |
| Self-employed hotel and restaurant owners | N/A | 36,100 | 14,700 |
| Shop, hotel and restaurant managers | 25,500 | 51,000 | 21,800 |

| | | | |
|---|---|---|---|
| Teachers | 26,600 | 54,300 | 22,400 |
| Science, engineering and ICT technicians | 29,000 | 50,300 | 21,400 |
| Health associate professionals (e.g. nurses) | 22,000 | 47,100 | 20,300 |
| Sales and administration associate professionals (e.g. accountants) | 26,900 | 52,600 | 22,700 |
| Legal and social associate professionnals | 19,500 | 43,900 | 18,800 |
| Non-commissioned officers | 31,500 | 44,600 | 17,800 |
| Shopkeepers | N/A | 36,200 | 15,500 |
| Office workers | 20,300 | 44,200 | 19,400 |
| Receptionists and customer service clerks | 17,600 | 42,600 | 18,900 |
| Police officers, armed service personnel and security agents | 22,700 | 37,400 | 16,700 |
| **Total middle class** | **23,600** | **46,300** | **20,200** |
| Farmers | N/A | 18,900 | 6,900 |
| Craftsmen | N/A | 28,800 | 12,000 |
| Nursing assistants, childcare workers, home-care assistants | 12,800 | 34,800 | 16,000 |
| Skilled construction workers | 13,000 | 27,200 | 11,400 |
| Skilled craft or food and drink industry workers | 11,300 | 28,700 | 12,100 |
| Workers in the metalwork and electronics industries | 21,200 | 37,100 | 15,400 |
| Machine operators | 14,600 | 33,400 | 14,200 |
| Drivers | 18,000 | 32,500 | 13,900 |
| Retail and service assistants | 11,200 | 31,200 | 14,000 |
| Manual labourers | 8,500 | 25,100 | 11,400 |
| Cleaners | 8,700 | 26,300 | 12,200 |
| Farm workers | 11,700 | 30,000 | 13,500 |
| **Total working class** | **12,500** | **26,600** | **13,000** |

*Source*: EU-SILC 2014. Populations: column 2: people in work aged between twenty-five and sixty-five, EU 27 (excluding Malta and Slovenia); columns 3 and 4: people in work aged between twenty-five and sixty-five, EU 27 (excluding Malta and Slovenia). Interpretation: in 2014, the median gross annual income of senior managers in Europe was €42,100 (expressed in purchasing-power parity and known as the purchasing-power standard in the EU). Senior managers in Europe are among those with a median total gross household income of €72,300 (PPP), and a median equivalised disposable income of €29,300 (PPP). Notes: gross household income corresponds to the combined gross income of the individuals in the household, to which is added social allowances, such as child support or housing assistance, and income from capital. Equivalised disposable income is the total household income of a household after taxes and other deductions, available to be spent or saved, divided by the number of members of the household converted into adult equivalents. Gross household income varies particularly widely where the respondents are agricultural workers, especially in Ireland. These results reflect the differing ways in which data on income are collected, and the distinction, which is more or less marked according to country, between self-employed farmers and those employed in farms in which they have part ownership.

One of the most significant developments in contemporary capitalism is undoubtedly the emergence, and now the increasing numbers, of people working in finance who earn huge salaries and whose job, rather than supervising people or products, is to manage capital flows.[9] The members of this tiny international elite, whose income has increased exponentially in recent years, are still too few to make a significant impact on randomly collected samples. The differences we point to here are somewhat approximate: being unable to give a full account of the extent of the divergences between the super-rich and others, European surveys have focused primarily on the inequality between the dominant class and other classes while highlighting the internal divisions within them.

For the majority of the population, standard of living depends primarily on the income each individual member of the household

---

9   Olivier Godechot, 'Is Finance Responsible for the Rise in Wage Inequality in France?', *Socio-economic Review* 10: 3, 2012, 447.

derives from work (whether they are employed or self-employed).[10] Looked at in terms of work income alone, the boundaries between the different classes may seem somewhat permeable: over the EU as a whole, the highest-paid 25 per cent in the middle class earn as much as the lower half of the dominant class. From this perspective, the upper part of the middle class is on a comparable level with the majority of the dominant class. The differences are more pronounced when we take into account the multiple components of financial capital, including income from assets which may be in the form of bonds, stock dividends or interest on savings.

With regard to income from work, the disparities within the dominant class – which vary widely both between individuals and between countries across the EU – are greater than those found among the classes lower down the social hierarchy. Disparities in income among self-employed people are even greater than among employees. However, it is difficult to compare self-employment income across countries in Europe. Yet even if we take into account only the income of employees, considerable differences emerge. Half of the members of the dominant class state a gross salary three times higher than the mean working-class salary (Table 11).

The upper layer of employees in Europe is bounded at one end by lawyers, judges, journalists and artists, whose median declared annual income is €26,000, and at the other by senior managers, with a median annual income of €42,100. This significant difference is nevertheless understated, for two reasons. First, benefits in kind or in the form of bonuses or stock options variable over time are not necessarily declared in statistical surveys. More broadly, the higher and more diversified the income, the greater the tendency for individuals to under-report this income. When the

10   With regard to the income figures in the EU-SILC survey, most countries collected data from household surveys. However, Finland, the Netherlands, Norway and Sweden relied on administrative records, supplemented by interviews with representative household members. See Maria Iacovou, Olena Kaminska and Horacio Levy, 'Using EU-SILC Data for Cross-national Analysis: Strengths, Problems and Recommendations', ESRC, ISER working paper, 2012.

country of origin of these revenues is not the country of residence, they are even less likely to declare them in their home jurisdiction. Second, when gross salaries are compared to gross household income and to disposable income, the dominant class's abilities to control how it defines its income, and thus to remain, on paper, somewhat vague about the nature and exact amount of its income, becomes apparent.

While the dominant class clearly sits above other classes in terms of income from work, this does not extend equally to both men and women. The gender pay gap has reduced somewhat since the onset of the crisis, falling from 17.3 per cent in 2008 to 16.2 per cent in 2011.[11] This gap, however, remains substantial and varies in magnitude across the different social classes. Male employees in the dominant class earn significantly more than women, reporting a median annual salary of €40,000, compared to only €28,000 reported by women in the same class, i.e. a €12,000 gap. In the middle and working classes, this gap is approximately €7,500 per year. These discrepancies, obviously, reveal institutional sexism and discrimination in career and promotion rules. Women are particularly affected by career breaks and by the 'glass ceiling' that prevents them from rising to positions at the top.

In addition to income from work, the dominant class also has other types of income. First there is the income from shares and other equity capital. A full 64 per cent of members of the dominant class have floating capital, revealing that at the top of the social ladder a connection exists between economic elites and those in possession of financial capital. Income from property, i.e. from renting land or buildings, is another characteristic of the wealthy in Europe, with 12 per cent of households in the dominant class stating that they receive such income. Those most likely to earn income from property include business owners (chief executive officers), 20 per cent of whom receive it. Taking into account these different components of financial capital, a social hierarchy can be drawn up on the basis of income declared in surveys (Table 11).

11    Francesca Bettio, Janneke Plantenga and Mark Smith, *Gender and the European Labour Market*, London: Routledge, 2013.

Senior managers report the most substantial financial resources, followed by doctors and health specialists, then engineers and specialists in science, engineering and information technology; the median gross household income of these groups taken together is above €60,000 per annum. This hierarchy is confirmed by reported disposable income, i.e. income after deduction of taxes and social-security contributions.

Being somewhat imprecise on issues relating to the top of the social hierarchy, the EU-SILC survey fails to highlight the separation of a tiny, predominantly male, section of the dominant class which, despite having comparable qualifications to the rest of their class, has enjoyed exponential salary increases. In the United Kingdom, for instance, the top percentile earned three times the median salary in 1970; today, this figure is more than five times greater.[12] The same is true of Ireland, where the share of wealth monopolised by the richest 1 per cent increased by 10 per cent in the 1990s and by 12.5 per cent over the 1990–2006 period.[13] This dizzying rise was ultimately halted, albeit very temporarily, by the 2008 crisis.

This rise in income inequality to the advantage of the dominant class is often justified by reference to their great responsibilities and associated risks. Yet this is not the picture that emerges from European surveys. To be sure, in 2010, large numbers of business and administration professionals (45 per cent) and senior managers (57 per cent) declared that an error in their work would cause their organisation financial losses. But exposure to the risk of error is in no way limited to the dominant class: for instance, similar proportions of drivers (51 per cent) and machine operators (58 per cent) gave the same response. Moreover, for these workers, exposure to risk does not mean the same as it does for those in the dominant

---

12   Anthony Atkinson and Sarah Voitchovsky, 'The Distribution of Top Earnings in the UK since the Second World War', *Economica* 78: 311, 2011, 440–59.

13   Brian Nolan, 'Long-Term Trends in Top Income Shares in Ireland', in Anthony Atkinson and Thomas Piketty (eds), *Top Incomes over the Twentieth Century: A Contrast between Continental European and English-Speaking Countries*, Oxford: Oxford University Press, 2007, 501–30.

class. For the dominant class, risk-taking cannot be dissociated from their position of responsibility with regard to the organisation of work, and this constitutes the best guarantee for the individual of protection against the consequences that an error might generate for the company. Risk-taking can even translate into cold, hard cash: in large corporations and financial institutions, risks generating positive results are remunerated with bonuses and stock options; if losses are incurred, the senior manager can always count on his/her basic salary. Risk-taking is a very different matter for subordinates, for whom it carries the threat of a direct sanction against the individual responsible in the event of a mistake.

While the alleged greater exposure to risk is an argument often put forward to justify the widening pay differentials, this is only one element in the financial dominance of the dominant class. European statistical surveys do not measure inequalities in assets, despite the fact that these inequalities are greater than those of income and are, moreover, cumulative. These different forms of social reproduction do still require some form of justification – a legitimacy that is expressed in other registers, such as cultural capacities and academic merit.

## THE THREE FORMS OF CULTURAL DISTINCTION OF THE DOMINANT CLASS

While financial capital remains the primary and most evident feature of the hegemony of the dominant class, this alone is insufficient to establish an authority perceived as legitimate by the entire society. Pierre Bourdieu showed that possession of academic credentials and the display of distinctive cultural practices represent ways of concealing the arbitrariness of dominance.[14] But to what extent can this mechanism, rooted in the French society of the second half of the twentieth century, be transposed to modern-day Europe?

14  Pierre Bourdieu, *Pascalian Meditations*, Stanford: Stanford University Press, 2000.

*The preservation of academic supremacy at all costs*

The academic capital of the dominant class is markedly higher than that of the other classes in the EU. More than three-quarters of the members of the dominant class in Europe have higher education qualifications, compared to 41 per cent of members of the middle class and 9 per cent of those in the working class. Many, indeed, are exceptionally highly qualified, with 44 per cent holding a master's degree or doctorate. Conversely, very few have been able to climb up the social ladder without the educational key that unlocks the door: people who did not complete secondary education make up barely 3 per cent of the dominant class. Within the dominant class, the most highly qualified are not necessarily the richest. Among senior managers at the top of the salary hierarchy, 37 per cent have a master's degree or doctorate, compared to 58 per cent of legal and social professionals, and approximately 50 per cent of doctors, health specialists and engineers. Only one in five chief executive officers has attained this level of education.

The weight of academic qualifications offers powerful protection against precarity and unemployment, which have affected only 3 per cent of the members of the dominant class. In 2013, the average unemployment rate of Europeans whose level of education was less than or equivalent to lower secondary education was 19 per cent, compared to 6 per cent for those with higher education qualifications.[15] Beyond protection against social insecurity, what academic resources particularly provide to the dominant class are knowledges, orientations towards certain cultural goods, and distinctive tendencies that make this a homogeneous group despite the variations between professions and between countries.

In the countries of the former Eastern Bloc, a higher education qualification is essential for those wishing to accede to management positions, and is thus a crucial issue for young people in these countries, where the socialist regime minimised other forms of social selection. However, access to higher education is also decisive in the social reproduction of the dominant class in the countries of Northern and Western Europe. Here, the expansion of

15   Eurostat, June 2014.

higher education in recent years has even reinforced the significance of strictly academic criteria, by making it harder to convert
inherited social capital into academic success. Surveys aiming to
identify the diverse variables that explain students' academic
success have revealed wide variations from country to country. In
Finland, 40 per cent of disadvantaged students achieve results that
place them among the top 25 per cent of best-performing students,
whereas the same is true for only 19 per cent of such students in
Hungary and 28 per cent in France.[16] These differences may be due
to the distribution of academic resources, to the time devoted to
learning, and even to early segregation of students into different
school pathways. The fact remains that the transmission of cultural
capital is no longer sufficient to access the most lucrative academic
qualifications.

Today, members of the dominant class do not need only to
make distinctive choices such as more selective and internationalised courses, or the accumulation of several qualifications, but also
to make financial investments – enrolment in private schools, individual tutoring – in the hope of subsequently realising their value
on the labour market. In countries such as the United Kingdom,
where school education is often private and costly, financial capital
is a decisive and indispensable advantage. As a result, there has
been, since the 1980s, a sharp rise in the amount spent on education among the British elite.[17] Broadly speaking, this 'service
expenditure' has even become distinctive of these classes, replacing previous forms of the conspicuous consumption of durable
goods, clothing, wine and fine food. These new distinctions have
widened inequalities, which have, however, become less visible in
the public arena.

In countries where education has remained public and affordable, the educational strategies of the dominant class also entail

---

16   OCDE, *PISA 2015 Results, Volume I: Excellence and Equity in
Education*, 2016.

17   Shinobu Majima and Alan Warde, 'Elite Consumption in Britain, 1961–
2004: Results of a Preliminary Investigation', *Sociological Review* 56: 1, 2008,
240–59.

drawing on financial resources, because they choose places of residence that facilitate access to the best schools. These strategies are also deployed on other levels, especially when it comes to accessing the most selective and prestigious institutions. In Sweden, where transmission of cultural capital across several generations remains the key driver of social reproduction,[18] members of the dominant class have turned to courses that incorporate high cultural values such as theatre, music, media, the ability to manage social relationships and the mastery of international skills (languages, classes taught in foreign languages). Through this, they seek to acquire international expertise and social resources rather than a more classical or scientific culture. This capital is valued because it enables access to high-ranking international public positions for those trained in law and political science, and to management positions for those trained in economics.[19]

The crucial factor, however, remains the accumulation of academic resources. In the Netherlands, the pre-university educational choices of the dominant class are markedly different from those of the middle and working classes, prioritising classic (*gymnasium*) and internationalised courses.[20] There are as many children of entrepreneurs as there are of senior managers and intellectual professionals enrolled in programmes promoting classical culture. The higher one climbs up the social hierarchy, the more tightly entwined financial and cultural capital become. One survey of Sweden's richest 1 per cent reveals the self-reinforcing and legitimising mechanisms of the wealthiest people through the accumulation of meritocratic signs. With the exception of the

---

18   Thomas Johansson, 'The Construction of the New Father: How Middle-Class Men Become Present Fathers', *International Review of Modern Sociology* 37: 1, 2011, 111–26.

19   Mikael Börjesson and Donald Broady, 'Elite Strategies in a Unified System of Higher Education: The Case of Sweden', *L'année sociologique* 66: 1, 2016, 115–46.

20   Don Weenink, 'Les stratégies éducatives des classes supérieures néerlandaises: Professions intellectuelles supérieures, managers et entrepreneurs face au choix entre capital culturel "classique" et capital culturel cosmopolite', *Actes de la recherche en sciences sociales* 191–2, 2012, 28–39.

independently wealthy, the different sections of these elites are characterised by an intensive investment in education across several generations.[21] Tellingly, the financial elite in Sweden is the group that has also invested most in academic capital, more even than the academic elite – proof, if proof were needed, that the economic dominance of the uppermost section of the dominant class is accompanied by a naturalisation of their material advantages through the symbolic recognition of their superiority.

The expansion of access to higher education for the most recent generations has thus obliged members of the dominant class to acquire specific and selective qualifications in order to maintain their dominant social position. While this competition seems to favour those who can invest the greatest resources in education, it also leads to the emergence of a series of smaller strategies of distinction that influence cultural practices.

## A legitimised and integrated cultural open-mindedness

Cultural capital is not limited to the mere possession of qualifications. It also refers to a set of orientations in recreational, entertainment and cultural practices. The few European surveys that make reference to social position provide only limited indicators on cultural capital, but analysis of a number of practices enables us to assess the magnitude of cultural inequalities.

In all countries across Europe, the dominant class is overrepresented among the most assiduous consumers of cultural activities: their members go to the cinema, to live performances and to cultural locations more often than Europeans in other social groups. They are distinguished from other classes especially in the area of cultural visits and attendance at performances. These practices become more intensive as level of education and income increase. While one-third of working-class people in Europe state that they attended at least one performance in the last year, the figure is 69 per cent for the dominant class (Table 12).

---

21    Andreas Melldahl, 'Modes of Reproduction in the Swedish Economic Elite: Education Strategies of the Children of the One Per Cent', *European Societies* 20: 3, 2018, 424–52.

*Table 12. Intensity of Leisure Practices in Europe*

| | No performance per year | At least one performance per year | Of which, more than three performances per year | No visit to cultural locations per year | At least one visit per year | Of which, more than three visits to cultural locations per year |
|---|---|---|---|---|---|---|
| Chief executive officers | 45% | 55% | 21% | 42% | 58% | 24% |
| Senior managers | 30% | 70% | 28% | 26% | 75% | 35% |
| Engineers and specialists in science, engineering and information technology | 34% | 66% | 25% | 26% | 74% | 33% |
| Doctors and health specialists | 26% | 74% | 31% | 24% | 76% | 37% |
| Administration, finance and business managers | 25% | 75% | 28% | 22% | 78% | 36% |
| Lawyers, judges, journalists, artists | 28% | 72% | 33% | 24% | 76% | 37% |
| Total dominant class | 31% | 69% | 28% | 26% | 74% | 34% |
| Total middle class | 42% | 58% | 19% | 41% | 59% | 22% |
| Total working class | 66% | 34% | 8% | 66% | 34% | 9% |

*Source*: EU-SILC 2006. *Population*: People in work aged between twenty-five and sixty-five, EU 27 (excluding Bulgaria, Ireland, Malta, the Netherlands and Romania). Interpretation: 70 per cent of senior managers attended a performance in the last twelve months. Note: data from Ireland and the Netherlands were excluded from the population because of a low response rate.

Even greater inequalities are apparent when we consider regular or one-off visits to cultural locations. Three-quarters of the members of the dominant class stated that they had visited at least one cultural location in the last twelve months, compared to six out of ten members of the middle class and one out of three members of the working class. Unfortunately, European sources provide no information about the content and practice of cultural activities, making it impossible to identify distinctive practices common to the same subgroup in a given class. This more in-depth analysis is only possible at the national level. In a study among the residents of Aalborg,[22] Denmark's third-largest city, researchers first identified a division between people with low cultural capital, who seldom read books or newspapers, and others, whose access to cultural consumption increases with their level of educational qualification. Among the 83 per cent of respondents who state that they read a newspaper, two distinct groups emerge: on the one hand, a minority which reads 'serious' newspapers offering political analysis and international news, on the other, those who prefer mass-appeal dailies, which are also popular among the most educated people.

If we limit analysis to the intensity of these cultural practices, the distance between social groups is sometimes small. In the dominant class, chief executive officers are distinguished by their low level of engagement in cultural activities, with 45 per cent of them not attending any performances and 42 per cent of them visiting no cultural sites in the past year, compared to a figure of 25 per cent of doctors. Within the middle class, on the other hand, teachers were much more likely to be engaged in cultural activities: three-quarters of them had seen a show and 80 per cent had visited a cultural site in the past year, placing them on the same level as judges and lawyers in terms of cultural practices. Thus, in their leisure practices, the most highly qualified sections of the middle class are close to

22   Annick Prieur, Lennart Rosenlund and Jacob Skjott-Larsen, 'Cultural Capital Today: A Case Study from Denmark', *Poetics* 36: 1, 2008, 45–71.

the cultural subgroup of the dominant class. The hierarchy of cultural practices does not therefore coincide exactly with the hierarchy of financial wealth, with some groups positioned higher or lower on one or other of these scales. In the United Kingdom, senior managers' investment in cultural activities, in particular the most highly regarded ones (theatre, opera, art galleries) also represents a means of maintaining and accumulating professional relationships, and thus an integral part of 'business'. These cultural practices are increasingly viewed as a continuation of the work undertaken with colleagues and clients.[23]

These observations thus raise the question of internal distinctions within the dominant class between a financial elite and a cultural elite. The Aalborg survey shows that, between 1980 and 2000, the occupations most associated with cultural capital, such as the scientific professions and teachers, experienced a decrease in purchasing power even as that of other social categories in the dominant class rose.[24] It may seem paradoxical that the positions held by some of the intellectual and artistic professions are being weakened at a time when the economy, especially in Northern and Western Europe, is increasingly turning towards the production of symbolic and cultural goods. Indeed, alongside the financial sector, a new sector of capitalism has emerged comprising activities such as the luxury goods industry, cultural tourism, the art market and the transformation of buildings or areas of landscape into national heritage.[25] This economy, which is oriented primarily towards the rich, relies heavily on the work of highly educated yet harshly exploited creators and producers of cultural content. These 'precarious intellectual workers', who live in cities such as London, Berlin, Vienna, Amsterdam and Paris, practise

23   Alan Warde and Tony Benett, 'A Culture in Common: The Cultural Consumption of the UK Managerial Elite', *Sociological Review* 56: 1, 2008, 240–59.

24   Prieur, Rosenlund and Skjott-Larsen, 'Cultural Capital Today'.

25   Luc Boltanski and Arnaud Esquerre, *Enrichissement: Une critique de la marchandise*, Paris: Gallimard, 2017.

diverse occupations (journalists, visual artists, researchers, web designers, etc.) but share specific forms of precarity: being forced to work freelance, they lack job security, and the boundaries between work and leisure activities are often blurred, leading to long and unsocial working hours, and considerable inequalities in income. In international surveys, part of this cluster appears in the category of creative and performing artists: compared to other members of the dominant class, artists are more likely to state that they work part-time (28 per cent versus 11 per cent on average) or on fixed-term contracts (31 per cent versus 8 per cent), or that they have a second job (13 per cent versus 5 per cent). These forms of precarity are not necessarily accompanied by low income, and they also affect other intellectual professions such as writers, journalists and researchers.

The increase in inequality is thus no longer apparent purely in the gaps between social groups. Within the dominant class itself, high-level qualifications do not protect against certain forms of marginalisation and self-exploitation. This reconfiguration of power relations may even be intensified by inequality of access to international resources.

*Acquisition of international skills and resources*
The cultural dominance of the dominant class relies on the mastery of skills and knowledge which enable its members to travel across borders with ease. These resources, which are conducive to international mobility, can then be reinvested and drawn upon in the national social space.

Often quick to advocate tolerance and openness to the world, in terms of their composition the dominant class is actually not very open to non-European foreigners, far less so than the working class (see Chapter 1). Yet its members do not remain confined within their national space. Their openness towards the world beyond their national borders takes other forms: whether they work for major corporations or as senior public servants in national and European administrations, members of the dominant class are increasingly offered opportunities to interact with their counterparts in other countries.

The internationalisation of the dominant class plays out primarily in the arena of leisure and professional sociability. Various indicators attest to this: fluency in several languages, contacts abroad, choosing to spend their holidays far from home, and exchanges with foreign colleagues in the workplace. While the practice of taking holidays abroad has become relatively democratised thanks to the development of low-cost airlines, it remains the privilege of the better-off. International mobility in the professional sphere is still limited to company directors, senior managers, senior civil servants, researchers and those in higher education aiming to enter these highly qualified professions. This mobility is a crucial resource that offers access to information and to particular institutional networks.[26] The EU also subsidises international mobility, for instance through the Erasmus programme, which offers international scholarships (in 2012–13, 270,000 students benefited from the programme).[27] Members of the dominant class thus acquire cosmopolitan resources which, after a long period during which they were perceived as remarkable, now represent a source of decisive legitimacy enabling access to positions of power within national borders and beyond.

The dominant class's openness to the wider world goes beyond mobility for business or leisure purposes. It is also rooted in the acquisition of an international culture that is today a distinctive feature of this social class. It involves the incorporation of genuine linguistic competence that allows easier access to other cultural realms. Knowledge of English, or of so-called 'international' languages such as Spanish and Russian, is a requirement of academic and professional success (Table 13).

26   Anthony Elliott and John Urry, *Mobile Lives*, London: Routledge, 2010, 11.

27   European Commission, 'Another Record-Breaking Year for Erasmus', July 2014.

*Table 13. Mastery of Foreign Languages in Europe*

| 'Which international language do you know best?' | No international language | English | Only one other international language (Spanish, Russian, etc.) |
|---|---|---|---|
| Dominant class | 12% | 67% | 21% |
| Middle class | 23% | 54% | 23% |
| Working class | 47% | 28% | 25% |
| Total | 32% | 45% | 23% |

*Source*: AES 2011. *Population*: People in work aged between twenty-five and sixty-five, EU 27 (excluding United Kingdom, Ireland and Malta). Interpretation: of languages spoken other than the native language, 67 per cent of the dominant class stated that English was the foreign language they knew best.

Linguistic capital is very unevenly distributed. One-third of Europeans do not speak any 'international' language other than their mother tongue; 45 per cent speak English, and 23 per cent speak another 'international' language such as Spanish or Russian. There is a structural opposition between those who do not speak any international language and those who speak English: two-thirds of the dominant class, and half of the middle class, state that they speak English, compared to only 28 per cent of the working class.[28] The divide is particularly great between intellectual and scientific occupations on the one hand (66 per cent speak English) and skilled manual workers, low-skilled white-collar workers and small-scale self-employed people on the other (less than 30 per cent). Although there is also a generational divide in language skills (75 per cent of young people compared to 58 per cent of older members of the dominant class; 40 per cent of young people compared to 20 per cent of older members of the working class), the class divide remains the strongest. There are also sharp differences between countries in the command of English, related to each country's political and economic history (whether they

28  Britain and Ireland are not included in these figures.

opened to trade earlier or later), size and education system. Residents of small countries such as Luxembourg or the Netherlands are more likely to speak a second language. Similarly, in the Scandinavian and Baltic countries, more than two-thirds of the population speak English. In Spain, Portugal and Austria, however, fewer people speak a second language.

The multiple professional and cultural exchanges of members of the dominant class on the international scene have led it to identify with the European project to a greater extent than other social groups. According to the Eurobarometer survey, Europeans with a high level of education and a high income have a more positive attitude towards the European Union. This is why Fligstein argues that Europe is a class project that favours the educated, self-employed senior managers and senior managerial employees.[29]

## FROM SOCIAL TO POLITICAL DOMINANCE

The accumulated weight of cultural and financial capital is evident well beyond the spheres of consumption and professional activity. This capital can be converted into positions of influence in the various spaces of representation across Europe. Reaching elected office at both state and European levels often requires academic qualifications and integration into particular social milieux, social networks or even financial resources, and this works to the advantage of those who already have or are able to access these resources. Thus the distribution of political power is structured around social position and helps to reproduce the dominance of the dominant class.

### The monopolisation of political representation

The first trend observed across all European countries is the almost total exclusion of the working class from politics at national level, and still more from the spheres of influence at the European Commission. Except under the old system in the countries of the former Eastern Bloc, manual workers and unskilled white-collar

29  Fligstein, *Euro-Clash*, 156.

workers have always been poorly represented among politicians at national level; even when they are present, it is in proportions that fall far short of representing their actual weight in European societies. But the striking fact of the last thirty years has been their almost total disappearance from parliaments. In the 2000s, in most national parliaments, fewer than 4 per cent of seats were held by working-class people.[30] Even in the countries of the former Eastern Bloc, it became rare for manual workers to be elected during the 1990s: in Hungary, for example, barely 2 per cent of seats were held by manual workers. In the European Parliament, there are no manual workers at all, and barely 2 per cent of MEPs were formerly low-skilled white-collar workers.[31] The disappearance of the working class from all political representation is largely due to the transformation of the parliamentary left, which from the beginning of the twentieth century until the 1960s–1970s had enabled working-class people to enter national parliaments. As a matter of principle, communist parties have long prioritised working-class candidates, but these parties have experienced a sharp decline, and even when they have maintained their presence their elected representatives now come mainly from the middle class, especially the public sector. Social-democratic parties, which have their roots in the working class, have for a long time increasingly made way for elected representatives from the upper middle class or even the dominant class. Politicians in Europe now form a group from which the working class are excluded.

As a result, the middle class, and still more the dominant class, now dominate political representation at both national and European levels. This monopoly on representative office has been

30   Heinrich Best and Maurizio Cotta (eds.), *Parliamentary Representatives in Europe 1848–2000: Legislative Recruitment and Careers in Eleven European Countries*, Oxford: Oxford University Press, 2000; Heinrich Best and Maurizio Cotta (eds.), *Democratic Representation in Europe: Diversity, Change and Convergence*, Oxford: Oxford University Press, 2007.

31   Willy Beauvallet, Victor Lepaux and Sébastien Michon, 'Qui sont les eurodéputés?', *Etudes européennes: La revue permanente des professionnels de l'Europe*, 2012, 1–14.

reinforced by the increasing importance of academic qualifications in achieving leadership roles in political parties, an essential first step for those seeking to be elected at the regional or national level. While the general level of education in Europe has risen since the 1960s, those holding higher education qualifications remain over-represented in the political arena and this trend is observed throughout Europe. On average, 70 per cent of national parliamentary representatives in Europe have university degrees,[32] and this is true even for the countries of Central and Eastern Europe.[33] In the European Parliament, one in every two MEPs has at least a master's degree, and almost one-fifth graduated abroad, strong evidence that there is a link between possession of cultural capital and cosmopolitan resources.

The role of academic qualifications in paving the way to elected political office is a major factor in the social homogeneity of those recruited, to the clear advantage of middle-class and dominant-class people working in the public sector. In the 2000s, on average 40 per cent of representatives in national parliaments had been public-sector employees. Many of these, particularly in the social-democratic parties, came from the teaching professions, which alone contributed close to 20 per cent of elected representatives in Western European countries,[34] and a little less in the countries of the former Eastern Bloc; the proportion of university lecturers was much higher than that of schoolteachers. In Spain, Portugal and Hungary, although the working class forms the clear majority of the population, intellectual professions are represented in large numbers in the national assemblies.[35] In the European Parliament, academic professions are also better represented than schoolteachers and associated professionals. Indeed, since the beginning of the

32   Daniel Gaxie and Laurent Godmer, 'Cultural Capital and Political Selection: Educational Backgrounds of Parliamentarians', in Best and Cotta, *Democratic Representation in Europe*, 106–35.

33   Heinrich Best, Elena Semenova and Michael Edinger, *Parliamentary Elites in Central and Eastern Europe*, New York: Routledge, 2014.

34   Cotta, Tavares de Almeida and Le Roux, 'De serviteurs de l'Etat'.

35   Best and Cotta, *Democratic Representation in Europe*.

2000s, the position of teachers has seen a relative but unmistakable decline. Among the most highly qualified representatives coming from the public sector, a substantial proportion had been high-ranking civil servants. Private-sector managers play a more limited political role, which varies across countries. There is a substantial proportion of senior managers and business owners within conservative parties in many countries, particularly in France, Germany and the United Kingdom, as well as in countries of Central and Eastern Europe, where political parties are still dependent on the private funding that these businessmen provide. Overall, with a few exceptions such as Italy and Denmark, the spaces of political representation lean towards the dominant class. Across Europe as a whole, one in every two elected representatives belongs to the dominant class.

### Bureaucratic elites protected from the reforms they advocate

The political power of the dominant sections of the dominant class is reinforced by the positions their members hold at high levels of government, though this varies from country to country.[36] In Italy and Greece, high-ranking positions in the civil service are predominantly the province of children of middle-class parents. But elsewhere in Europe these positions are still the preserve of scions of the dominant class. While in Spain they are primarily occupied by members of the business elite, in Nordic countries they are concentrated among groups less closely aligned with financial elites. France and the United Kingdom offer the clearest illustration of this over-representation of the dominant class at high levels of government.[37] In the United Kingdom, senior civil servants are often alumni of Oxford or Cambridge, universities which are both highly socially selective. In France, this social selection is conducted

---

36   Edward C. Page and Vincent Wright, *Bureaucratic Elites in Western European States*, Oxford and New York: Oxford University Press, 1999.

37   Mairi MacLean, Charles Harvey and Robert Chia, 'Dominant Corporate Agents and the Power Elite in Spain and Britain', *Organization Studies* 31: 3, 2010, 327–48.

via the elite institutions Sciences Po Paris (Paris Institute of Political Studies) and the Ecole nationale d'administration (National School of Administration). In Germany, three-quarters of senior federal civil servants come from the dominant class, and they are often the sons and daughters of senior civil servants or of senior managers in the private sector. As for parliamentarians, high-level educational qualifications are required and there is an increasingly marked preference for economics rather than law degrees. The career pursued often culminates in the directorship of a government department or quango, and thus a very high salary even in countries such as Italy, where public service is otherwise not valued. State authority allows access to the highest social strata and the accumulation of different types of capital. In contrast to careers as elected officials and political representatives, senior government positions are monopolised by the dominant class, for whom they have become a means to reinforce social reproduction, notably in the context of the neoliberal turn during the 1980s.

Despite both the New Public Management reforms that began in Europe in the 1980s and the crisis in public finance after 2008, these national bureaucratic elites have managed to maintain their positions and have resisted the effects of their own state reforms particularly effectively. In some countries, such as Spain and France, senior civil servants have been exposed to relative wage restraint, but remained much better protected from the crisis than other categories of civil servants. Thus in the countries most affected by the crisis, such as Greece, but also Italy and Ireland, senior civil servants remain the only state employees to have escaped wage cuts.

Managerial reforms and the crisis have given rise to contrasting pay and career prospects within these elites, differentiating 'top management' from other civil servants. However, there are more and more opportunities to move between high public office and politics, and these encourage the concentration of power within an increasingly homogeneous and consistent group. In Spain, senior civil servants literally monopolise ministerial posts and the offices of secretaries of state. In a country marked by numerous political crises and weak parliaments, the bureaucratic elites have been able to ensure their own stability and survive changes of government, their social reproduction remaining undisturbed by the transition to democracy and shifts in political power. On the contrary, it is primarily among these elites that politicians have been recruited under both socialist and conservative governments. The widespread practice of 'special leave' allows them to take on political office without having to leave their administrative positions, and they thus continue to enjoy the benefits associated with these positions.[38]

The senior ranks of public administration in European institutions are of more recent origin, and are undoubtedly less homogeneous than the state elite at national level. The bureaucratic elites of Brussels also differ from the international financial bourgeoisie in that they owe their positions to their cultural capital and expert knowledge. This group is highly qualified (70 per cent have a higher education degree), primarily trained in the fields of economics, natural sciences and law, and internationalised (58 per cent have studied abroad).[39]

While the dominant sections of the dominant class are largely over-represented within senior public service, they also know how to delegate the defence of their interests to intermediaries, for a fee, and thus how to influence state authorities and policy. The adoption of certain tax arrangements offering exemption from general law, or the allocation of state aid to certain sectors, may, for instance, be analysed as indirect rewards for donations made by the richest to political campaign funds. The big bosses of European corporations even make the effort to entrust the work of defending

38   Alba Tercedor Carlos, 'Les élites administratives en Espagne: Vieilles inerties et nouveaux défis', *Revue française d'administration publique*, 151–52(3), 697–718.

See also Pedro Tavares de Almeida, António Costa Pinto and Nancy Bermeo (eds.), *Who Governs Southern Europe? Regime Change and Ministerial Recruitment, 1850–2000*, London: Frank Cass, 2003.

39   Hussein Kassim, John Peterson, Michael W. Bauer, Sara Connolly, Renaud Dehousse, Liesbet Hooghe and Andrew Thompson, *The European Commission of the Twenty-First Century*, Oxford: Oxford University Press, 2013.

and promoting their interests to highly paid professionals. Thus, while the European branch of Greenpeace, the largest citizen NGO, has a budget of €3.8 million, the chemical and pharmaceutical industry lobby can raise up to €40 million to defend their interests.[40] Working as lobbyists, experts and other consultants for firms, these 'shadow elites' act on the fringes of the state and wield considerable power,[41] actively influencing government decisions. Generally keeping their distance from media controversies and public events, their activity is invisible. Their strategy revolves entirely around constructing a 'quiet politics' that works through intervention and expertise with bureaucratic elites over the long term.[42] When it comes to influencing the European Commission, the financial elites can rely on an army of tiny hands dedicated to the defence of their interests.

Ultimately, this portrayal of the dominant class in Europe reveals its different facets as well as its similarities. Beyond its economically dominant position, this class is characterised by an accumulation of various resources disproportionate to those held by the middle and working classes of Europe.

Our results sketch out elements of compelling evidence of a convergence between the dominant classes in different countries of the European Union that is more marked than that observed among other social classes. This relative homogeneity is strongly reflected in the enthusiasm of a major proportion of the dominant class for the construction of the European Union. One study on European elites, which thus relates to a population smaller than the one we considered, suggests that the dominant class across Europe believes that the rise of nationalism is a threat and that the

40   Sylvain Laurens, *Lobbyists and Bureaucrats in Brussels: Capitalism's Brokers*, London: Routledge, 2017.

41   Janine R. Wedel, *Shadow Elites: How the World's New Power Brokers Undermine Democracy, Government, and the Free Market*, New York: Basic Books, 2010, 5.

42   Pepper D. Culpepper, *Quiet Politics and Business Power: Corporate Control in Europe and Japan*, New York: Cambridge University Press, 2011.

European Union must develop a genuinely shared foreign policy. It also believes that the primary role of the EU is to improve the competitiveness of businesses rather than the social protection of workers.

Intensive cultural practices, multilingualism and enthusiasm for the European project are common traits shared by most members of the dominant class. Looking at the uppermost part of the social space, one might be forgiven for thinking that national characteristics are fading away in favour of converging interests. However, elites in Central, Eastern and Southern Europe do not have the same relationship with European institutions, nor do they play the same political role within them. More generally, the majority of other Europeans consider that national borders have retained their significance and have even reinforced social barriers which remain very difficult to cross.

# 4

# Dominance and Exclusion: The Interplay between Social Class and Nation

Considered at the level of Europe as a whole, the three great social classes are less homogeneous than they are within each country. They outline a system of inequalities that plays out differently in different geographical regions. Nevertheless, nation states and their institutions still wield a powerful influence over the political construction of social groups: belonging to the working class, middle class or dominant class is not the same experience in Copenhagen as it is in Athens, the periurban zones of Austria or rural Hungary – notwithstanding their geographical proximity. A given social position as defined at the European level may encompass realities that differ substantially from one country to another. In Romania and Bulgaria, the working class largely comprises farmers and agricultural workers, whereas in the United Kingdom and Sweden it tends to be made up of unskilled workers. The dominant class in Greece includes a substantial number of doctors, whereas in Germany it consists predominantly of senior managers. It might be assumed that the unification of commodity markets and the freedom of movement for workers would soften these national differentiations. However, differences between social classes remain significant, and are even accentuated by the process of European construction.

The lack of a standardised social policy in Europe, and the refusal to regulate business relocations, have a significant influence on the system of inequalities: relations between classes are constantly being reconfigured, as a result of the exchanges and the economic and cultural power relations that are created between Europeans in the world of work and in other social spheres. The liberal policies that are being rolled out throughout Europe have widely varying consequences in different countries, and for different social groups. On the one hand, they offer the promise of cultural and economic opportunities for the dominant classes in the countries with the wealthiest economies. On the other, they intensify the massive increase in disadvantaged groups in the countries with the least economic power. In order to make this clear, we have chosen to consider each social class associated with a country as an entity in itself: the effects of policies of merging and the redeployment of large European corporations are not felt in the same way by the working class in Italy and in Poland; similarly, access to economic and cultural resources is not the same for the dominant class in Portugal as it is for those in Denmark. Within our consideration of the continent as a single social space, we have identified six overall social groups, composed of classes or sections of classes from several European countries.[1] This representation allows us to show concretely in what ways the social classes within each country resemble and are distinguished from one another at the European level, and come to form coherent groupings that are more or less aware of their common interests. In order to give an account of the power relations between classes and between countries, we have chosen to focus on the two extremes of the European social space. At the bottom of the European social pyramid, the working class of the South and the East is revealed in many ways as much more disadvantaged than the equivalent group in the rest of Europe. At the top of the pyramid, the dominant class of the countries of the North enjoy complete supremacy. The increasing number of spaces where these groups encounter one another in the European arena makes the contrast between these two extremes all the stronger: direct relations between individuals of different social groups are proliferating, through migration for work, of course, but also through student mobility and through tourism.

---

1   For more detail on how these social groups are identified within the European social space, see Appendix 4.

## AT THE BOTTOM OF THE EUROPEAN SOCIAL SPACE

Over the last thirty years, the economic and social equilibriums that previously held sway in Europe have been progressively modified as the EU expanded to include new member states. Historically, there was a structural divide between the rich nations of the North, including those that initiated the European project, and those of the South, which were brought in more recently. Since the entry of the former countries of the East into the European Union, this structural opposition has been overturned. It is now the working class in the eastern part of the continent which forms the base of the European social space, albeit with internal variations: Hungary, Poland and the Czech Republic have seen strong economic development, while Bulgaria and Romania are still characterised by great poverty. For their part, the workers in the countries of the South, such as Portugal and Greece, are on a socio-economic level substantially higher than that of their peers in Central and Eastern Europe, but bear the full force of the austerity policies that Brussels enforces as a condition of their staying in the European Union.

*The working class of the East and South: the dogsbodies of Europe*
In many respects, the working class in the countries of the East and South occupies the lowest position in the European social space, and shows signs of great financial poverty, combined with working conditions that are harsher than anywhere else.[2] Moreover, the statistical surveys available relate only to people in employment, resulting in an underestimate of the difficulties encountered by the most marginalised groups, particularly those who make their living from the 'informal' economy.

This highly disadvantaged position in the job market is due in large part to the social shifts that have taken place in these countries in the last twenty years. In Romania, one of the most economically

2   For a similar observation based on substantially different indicators, see Frédéric Lebaron and Pierre Blavier, 'Classes et nations: Quelle articulation à l'échelle européenne', *Actes de la recherche en sciences sociales* 219, 2017, 80–97.

disadvantaged countries, the number of industrial jobs fell from 4.7 million in 1990 to 1.7 million in 2012. Redundancies in industrial and mining regions have forced many workers to return to the rural regions they came from, where they live at barely more than subsistence level. In the Jiu valley, restructuring in the mines has definitively broken the power of the miners, who formed the working-class aristocracy prior to the fall of Ceaușescu. This forced-march transition of the former industrial regions has resulted in deteriorating living standards and the destabilisation of home and family. While some emigrate – initially to Hungarian mines, later to other EU member countries following the 2007 enlargement – or start their own businesses, there are many former miners who are isolated in their homes. Through the drastic reduction in jobs resulting from voluntary redundancies, places of male sociality have become deserted, and local and family solidarities dislocated. The reduction in the status of workers has eroded the system of values associated with the mine, which extolled class loyalty and physical labour. The wives of ex-miners have been forced to look for work, usually of a highly precarious nature: agricultural day labour, short-term contracts in the cleaning and maintenance sectors, or retail jobs in the clothing industry and small-scale food production.[3]

Within each of the countries of Central and Eastern Europe, there is a hierarchy of exclusion.[4] But the working class in these countries, which sits at the base of the European social space, has been deeply affected by economic restructuring. The accelerated conversion to a capitalist economy has gone hand in hand with the loss of large numbers of industrial jobs and a collapse in agricultural activity in some regions. In the late 1990s, countries such as Poland and Bulgaria saw an unprecedented rise in undeclared work

---

3  Maria Voichiţa Grecu, '"On est resté l'écume du métier": Le groupe des mineurs de la vallée du Jiu (Roumanie) disloqué par les restructurations, 1997–2013', *Travail et emploi* 137, 2014, 123–38.

4  In 2014, for example, the annual income of working-class people in employment ranged from €6,500 in Romania to €12,700 in the Czech Republic, with Hungary in the middle at €8,600 (these figures are, of course, expressed in purchasing-power parity, i.e. corrected to take into account the wide disparities in the cost of living in different countries, in order to draw a meaningful comparison).

(classified by international organisations as 'informal'). This sector of the economy in the former countries of the East is difficult to evaluate: its share of GDP remains high, but the proportion of workers working in the informal sector has fallen, to the extent that with the exception of Poland, it is similar to that in the West. According to some studies, this is not the case in the countries of the South, particularly Greece, Cyprus and Portugal,[5] where undeclared work has continued to flourish owing to the rapid shifts in social structures:[6] still today, it is the only way that many households hit by the crisis manage to get by.

Until the 1970s, the working class in Portugal worked predominantly in agriculture, but over the space of thirty years the agricultural sector has shrunk, being replaced by manual work and particularly by unskilled white-collar jobs. This restructuring of the working class has been less centred on industry – which has been stagnant since the 1980s – than on the construction sector for men, and unskilled services for women. The rate of women's economic activity has risen from 29 per cent in 1970 to 65 per cent in 2001. The majority of working-class people in work now live in cities (38 per cent of the population lived in Lisbon and Oporto in the 2000s), with precarious conditions of work and employment that force regular migrations to neighbouring countries. In the cities, the growth of a skilled sector may offer some opportunities for mobility for the working class, but it is rarer in the rural areas of the country,

---

5   Mihail Hazans, 'Informal Workers across Europe: Evidence from 30 Countries', IZA discussion paper 5871, Bonn, Institute for the Study of Labor, 2011.

6   Other estimates of the informal economy in European countries offer a slightly different picture: amounting to approximately 18 per cent of GDP in Europe as a whole in 2015, it is thought to be high in the countries of the South (22 per cent of GDP in Greece, for example), but still higher in many countries of Central and Eastern Europe (31 per cent in Bulgaria, 28 per cent in Romania, 23 per cent in Poland, over 24 per cent in the Baltic countries). Friedrich Schneider, 'Size and Development of the Shadow Economy of 31 European and 5 other OECD Countries from 2003 to 2015: Different Developments', *Journal of Self-Governance and Management Economics* 3: 4, 2015, 7–29.

where social reproduction is still significant and levels of education remain fairly low.[7]

Although its situation is a little more favourable than that of the former countries of the East, the working class in the South of Europe is still very far removed from that of the rest of Europe: in Portugal and Greece, earned income among the working class hovers around €9,000, far below what its members might aspire to in Italy (€15,750), and only a third of average working-class income in Denmark (€28,000). It is easy to understand why almost the entirety of the Greek and Portuguese working class state that they find it difficult to make ends meet at the end of the month. By comparison, only half to one-third of the working class in Sweden, Denmark, Germany and the Netherlands describe this kind of financial fragility.

Over Europe as a whole, inequalities in living standards are intensified by the varying extent of systems of social protection. The consequences can be measured in the arena of access to healthcare: among the working class, one-quarter of Lithuanians, one-fifth of Portuguese and 17 per cent of Greeks report that for financial reasons they have been forced to go without a dental check-up they needed, whereas going without dental treatment is reported by only 3 per cent of the working class in Germany, the United Kingdom and the Netherlands. These disparities are due to differences in income, but also derive from the shortcomings of the state, which offers little in the way of social protection in the countries of the East and South of Europe. In Portugal, the serious difficulty in accessing healthcare combines with a high, and lasting, level of poverty, owing to the pitiful level of social-security benefits and compensation, in a country where state intervention in healthcare was only recently introduced.[8] In effect, the

7   José Madureira Pinto, 'Cultural and Educational Heritage, Social Structure and Quality of Life', in Guy Neave and Alberto Amaral (eds), *Higher Education in Portugal 1974–2009: A Nation, a Generation*, London: Palgrave, 2012, 89–107.

8   Alfredo Bruto da Costa, Ana Cardoso and Isabel Baptista, 'The Dynamics of Income Poverty and Social Exclusion in Portugal', in Eleni Apospori and Jane Millar (eds), *The Dynamics of Social Exclusion in Europe: Comparing Austria, Germany, Greece, Portugal and the UK*, Gloucester and Northampton: Edward Elgar Publishing, 2003, 114–38.

social-security system that was put in place after the 1974 revolution in Portugal leaves whole sectors of the working class without protection, while the dominant class benefit more from social-security payments than in other countries.[9] This increases the importance of family support. Following the 2008 crisis, in countries such as Greece and Portugal the drastic reduction in public spending on health imposed by the European Union resulted in the reactivation of informal mechanisms of mutual support between friends and relatives.

Thus the process of European integration has two faces: if we go only by macroeconomic national indicators, it presents as a relative narrowing of the gap between the countries of the East and South and the rest of Europe. But behind this deceptive image of overall increase in wealth, the economic changes have mainly benefited a minority, and have increased inequalities between regions.

### The destabilisation of the rural working class in the East

The accelerated transition of the former socialist countries to a market economy not only destroyed many jobs in industry but also radically transformed the conditions of access to the labour market: a high-school leaving certificate has now become an essential condition for entry to and remaining in employment, resulting in the relegation of entire generations of workers with little or no education to unemployment or inactivity. As we have already seen in relation to Romania, many have then been forced to return to rural areas, a factor that has helped to reinforce the economic disparity between urban and rural zones.

The social conditions of the rural working class are far from uniform throughout the countries of Central and Eastern Europe. In the Czech Republic and Hungary, for example, the farming population has continued to fall, while it has stayed relatively stable in Poland and Romania.[10] However, the reforms of the last twenty years have exacerbated inequalities, while redistributing

---

9   Leonor Vasconcelos Ferreira, 'Persistent Poverty: Portugal and the Southern European Welfare Regime', *European Societies* 10: 1, 2008, 49–71.

10   François Bafoil, *Central and Eastern Europe: Europeanization and Social Change*, New York: Palgrave Macmillan, 2009.

positions of power. In the Romanian village of Aurel Vlaicu, for example, the restoration of land to its former owners or their descendants, which was instituted in 1991 under pressure from international institutions, has inverted the relations of power between landowners and tenants.[11] To begin with, the former officials of the Ceauşescu regime who had been managing collective and state farms retained a monopoly on farm machinery. They were thus the only ones able to cultivate the land, and were able to dictate rent levels for farmland to the new small landowners. These 'supertenants' rapidly became the affluent class in the privatised Romanian countryside. Subsequently, in the late 1990s, they were in a position to buy land, and sold it to foreign investors, while remaining as managers of commercial farms. Thus, within the space of twenty years, the rural grandees of the former regime have managed to convert their power into economic capital. They have become the main beneficiaries of the economic changes resulting from the opening of the country to foreign investors, in rural zones hit by lasting unemployment, where many poor labourers nevertheless still manage to find a way to subsist. In 2014, 35 per cent of the Romanian working class and 22 per cent of their Polish counterparts worked in the agricultural sector, either self-employed or as employees. Most farms are small (averaging 3.5 hectares in Romania, 8.1 hectares in Poland), and small farmers still today make up substantial social groups: in 2014, they comprised 19 per cent of people in work in Romania (28 per cent of the working class) and 10 per cent of people in work in Poland (20 per cent of the working class). In the South, only Greece has as many farmers.

Over twenty-five years, the economic transition of the former countries of the East has thus pitched a large proportion of the rural working class into extreme poverty, while at the same time inculcating in them a sense of their own unworthiness. These pariahs of Europe now emerge as the people most excluded from the resources that enable access to the most everyday goods and facilities. For

11   Katherine Verdery, *The Vanishing Hectare: Property and Value in Postsocialist Transylvania*, Ithaca, NY: Cornell University Press, 2003.

example, four in ten working-class people in Bulgaria say they can only afford to eat meat or fish every other day, and one-third are in this position in Hungary. Such nutritional deprivation is almost unknown (between 2 and 5 per cent) among working-class households in Denmark, Spain, the Netherlands and Sweden. Ownership of domestic appliances reveals the same stark discrepancies: around 10 per cent of working-class people in Romania and Bulgaria state that they cannot afford a washing machine, whereas almost all Europeans in the West and North have one. The working class in Central and Eastern Europe thus finds itself permanently relegated to the paradox of the conquered: in a context of increasing valorisation of Western European lifestyles, it has to deal with the economic deprivation that prohibits access to them.

## The middle class in the East and South: the upper level of lower Europe

Many commentators, glossing over the devastating effects of the transition to capitalism, hail the emergence of a middle class in the former countries of the East and emphasise its stabilising role in societies undergoing reconstruction. They see this as an incontrovertible sign of economic prosperity, which they attribute to the market economy.[12] These reassuring discourses are in fact based on a series of misunderstandings: they incorporate the new elites born from the economic changes, such as entrepreneurs and senior managers in privatised enterprises, into the middle class, effectively postulating that no dominant class exists.

The figure of the entrepreneur is often wheeled out to represent the middle class in the countries of the East, presented as the symbol of a society being transformed in harmony with the ideals of tolerance and individual freedom.[13] However, the term 'entrepreneur' conceals a vast range of realities, from the company CEO to street hawkers, from newspaper vendors to the owners of garment

12   David Ost, 'Class after Communism: Introduction to the Special Issue', *East European Politics and Societies and Cultures* 29: 3, 2015, 543–64.

13   Henryk Domanski, *The Polish Middle Class* (2002), Frankfurt am Main: Peter Lang, 2015.

workshops. During the early years of transition to the market economy, many former manual workers may have seen entrepreneurship
as a path to some increase in social standing, and to greater personal
wealth: in the early 2000s, the Polish economy numbered nearly two
million single-ownership enterprises. But their economic situation
rapidly deteriorated, and starting one's own business now emerges
instead as a way of escaping unemployment or of supplementing
household income. In Poland, the number of self-employed workers
who state they have a second job is larger than elsewhere in Europe.

Far from the rosy images of a middle class taking advantage of
the new economic prospects, statistical studies show rather that
their resources are meagre, even compared to the most disadvantaged countries of the European South. At the bottom of the hierarchy are, once again, the Romanian middle class, which in 2014
drew a median annual income of €9,000 from their paid work;
above it came the middle class in Poland, at €15,500, and a little
higher in the country rankings, those of Greece and Portugal, at
around €16,500. These low salaries put them far behind the working class in Austria (€21,500) and Scandinavia (between €23,000
and €28,000). These middle classes which sit at the lower levels on
the European scale nevertheless have sufficient resources to distinguish them from the manual and unskilled white-collar workers
in their countries. Three-quarters of the middle class in Portugal
and Romania, and more than half in the Czech Republic and
Poland, report regularly finding themselves in financial difficulty,
putting them midway between the working class in the East and
that in the North of Europe, where this experience is much less
common. Their modest economic resources provide them with
limited but real access to leisure and cultural consumption. For
example, two-thirds of the Polish and Hungarian middle class can
afford one week's holiday per year, a proportion substantially
higher than that in the working class in their country, but well
below that among the Danish and Swedish working class, around
85 per cent of whom are able to go on holiday (see Graph 2). Only
in the Czech Republic do more than three-quarters of the middle
class go on holiday, placing them at the same level as the working
class in the countries of the North and West of Europe.

*Graph 2. Ability to Afford One Week's Holiday in Europe*

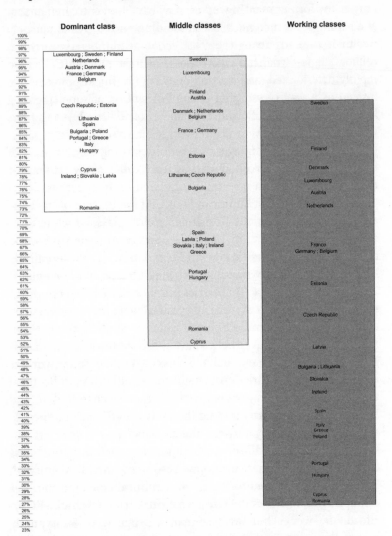

*Note*: Of people in work aged between twenty-five and sixty-five, EU 27 (excluding Malta and Slovenia), 97 per cent of the dominant class in Luxembourg state that they are able to afford one week's holiday, compared to 27 per cent of the working class in Romania. The rate of non-response in the United Kingdom is 11 per cent.
*Source*: EU-SILC 2014.

The middle classes in the countries of the East and South are also lower down the scale in terms of cultural practices: half of the Czech and Portuguese middle classes say they go to the cinema at least once a year, putting them above the working class in their country but below the working class in Denmark, six in ten of whose members say they have gone to the cinema. The figure for attendance at live performances indicates even starker discrepancy, and emphasises more strongly how close the middle class in the East and South come to the working class in the North and West. In Poland and the Czech Republic, the proportion of the middle class who have attended at least one live performance during the last year (40 per cent and 55 per cent respectively) is on a par with that among the working class in Germany (43 per cent), Denmark (49 per cent) and Sweden (53 per cent), while still remaining well above that among the working class in their own country (14 per cent and 26 per cent respectively). These indicators suggest that the middle classes in the countries of the East and South of Europe occupy an intermediate position in the European social class space: in a number of studies, they emerge as the top layer of the lower level in Europe, just above the bottom of the European social scale. With limited financial resources, they have a small amount of cultural capital that distinguishes them from the working class in their own country, but keeps them at a distance from cultural practices pertaining in the rest of Europe.

Focusing on the living standards and working conditions of people in work helps to give a more accurate measure of the discrepancies between one country and another, and their effects on the structure of the European social space. Notwithstanding optimistic pronouncements based on traditional economic performance indicators published by international institutions (the ECB, Eurostat, the OECD, the IMF), comparison of data by country and by social class shows that reduction in inequality is far from uniform through all levels of society. In the countries of the North and West, the working class has often been hit by unemployment, increased precarity of employment and deteriorating working conditions, while in the East and South of Europe it is distinguished by much lower wage levels and standards of living.

## THE HEGEMONY OF THE DOMINANT CLASS OF THE NORTH AND WEST

By contrast, the economic changes resulting from the unification of European markets have substantially benefited the dominant classes in Europe. These groups enjoy good working conditions, are at relatively low risk of unemployment, report diverse cultural practices and own comfortable homes. These distinctive characteristics extend this group beyond what some call the elite, but also make them more heterogeneous over Europe as a whole. There is a stark contrast between the dominant classes in the North and West, who are the most powerful in the whole of Europe, and those in the East and South, who are dominant at regional level. This is particularly true of the economic elites: those who constitute the core of European capitalism, the directors of European multinationals, are recruited primarily from France, Germany, the United Kingdom and sometimes the Nordic countries, but rarely from the countries of the South and never from Central and Eastern Europe.[14] This divide, measurable in the first instance in terms of income, is reinforced by other elements such as level of education, leisure and relation to work. In the countries of the West and North, the conspicuous leisure of the dominant class as described by Thorstein Veblen in the late nineteenth century seems a thing of the past:[15] commitment to work, alongside investment in cultural socialisation and education, has become the distinguishing characteristic of those at the top of the social hierarchy. In the countries of the East and South, investment in education also represents the main source of legitimacy of the dominant class.

### The key role of financial capital

The dominant classes in the various countries of Europe are distinguished first and foremost by level of salary.[16] Two quite

---

14   Philippe Blanchard, François-Xavier Dudouet and Antoine Vion, 'Le cœur des affaires de la zone euro', *Cultures and conflits* 98, 2015, 71–99.

15   Thorstein Veblen, *The Theory of the Leisure Class*, Abingdon: Routledge, (1899) 2017.

16   This measure is less accurate and probably less reliable than data extracted from declarations to tax authorities.

distinct worlds emerge here: while three-quarters of the dominant class in Denmark and Luxembourg are among the top 25 per cent of Europeans in terms of salary, this is the case for only 16 per cent of the dominant class in Greece, 15 per cent in Hungary and 6 per cent in Bulgaria. Whereas the median annual salary of the dominant class in France is €41,000, it is barely €20,000 in Hungary, €8,000 below the median annual salary of the working class in Scandinavia. These sharp income inequalities are due primarily to differences in the concentration of economic resources in different European countries. They are also linked to age differences: the dominant classes in the countries of Central and Eastern Europe – with the exception of Bulgaria – are on average younger than those in Denmark, France, Germany, Sweden and the Netherlands. An additional factor is the weight of income from sources other than work: while 90 per cent of the dominant class in France and Sweden earn income from investments (interest, dividends, profits on company shares), this is true of only 45 per cent of those in Portugal and only 13 per cent of those in Hungary. In terms of income, the dominant classes in Central and Eastern Europe fall well behind the middle class in the North and West.

Moreover, it appears that the dominant classes of the countries of the East and South evaluate their financial situation in comparison with the income of their counterparts in the North and West rather than on the scale of their own countries: among the dominant class, 44 per cent in Greece, 54 per cent in Hungary and 56 per cent in Portugal feel that they are well paid, compared to 70 per cent in Denmark, the Netherlands and Sweden. These differences have no impact on the ability to meet everyday needs, but do point to significant differences in modes of leisure. The issue of holidays is a good indicator of inequalities of class and between countries. Family size does, of course, play a part in the decision to go on holiday, but a breakdown by country and by social position offers a revealing overview of the differences between people from different parts of Europe. While almost all of the dominant classes in Sweden, Denmark and Finland state that they go on holiday every year, the proportions are 80 per cent in Hungary and less than 75 per cent in Romania. The choice of destination is also significant: in Scandinavia, the standard destination for travel is Europe or even further afield, while the dominant classes of the East tend more to stay in their own country.

The pre-eminence of the dominant class of the countries of the North and West can be measured not only in comparison with the eastern part of Europe, but also within each country: the median annual salary gap between the dominant class and the middle class is €15,000 in France and €16,700 in Germany, against only €7,500 in Sweden, the least unequal among the wealthy countries of Europe. This means, for example, that a German senior manager earns on average €21,000 more than a teacher. These income differences are exacerbated by the massive increase in remuneration for super-executives in the finance industry in Paris, London and Frankfurt: there are too few of these latter to be visible in European surveys, but they nevertheless factor heavily in the rise in inequality between East and West.

The dominance of the dominant class is not restricted to income; it is also based on financial and cultural capital that is passed down through families. But the ways in which this position of privilege is justified varies according to country. In some countries the work that these people do is advanced as evidence that they deserve it, in some the qualifications they have, and in others both are emphasised.

### Legitimisation of the dominant class of Northern Europe through work

For several decades now, the dominance of the dominant class in the countries of the North and West has been built on educational meritocracy rather than on claims to cultural or social superiority. Today, top-ranked academic institutions transmit both a legitimate culture that allows their alumni to distinguish themselves from the middle and working class, and the capacity to demonstrate wide-ranging tastes – being able to appreciate classical music and rap, arthouse or experimental films alongside television soap operas and so on. The focus is on learning to move in diverse cultural spaces, as a way of demonstrating one's originality and singularity.[17] Complementing this, commitment to work is also a register through which social and financial dominance is legitimised. In the United Kingdom, the dominant class justify their high salaries and good standard of living with the mantra, 'I worked hard for it.'[18] The European surveys offer a number of indications of this overvaluation of work, which now forms the basis for the legitimacy of the dominant class.

During the 1945–75 period, with the development of highly skilled jobs in large companies, managers came to form a substantial component of the dominant class, gradually supplanting the independently wealthy.[19] In France, managerial staff made up only 10 per cent of the working population in the early 1960s, and numbers only began to rise steeply during the 1970s. In the United Kingdom, the service class, which encompasses executives, higher intellectual professions and the most highly qualified of the intermediate professions, shows a similar dynamic.[20] In societies where increase in wealth is fed by economic growth, it has become essential for the dominant class to demonstrate their presence and engagement in work in order to justify their ascendancy in the productive sphere, as a number of indicators show. While working hours in general have fallen markedly in Western Europe, those of manual workers have decreased more rapidly, and they now work fewer hours than managers. This is not the case, however, in Central and Eastern Europe. What we are seeing here is a reversal of history: in France, Austria, Sweden, Germany, Belgium and the Netherlands, the proportion of senior managers and of intellectual and scientific professionals who state they work long weeks (more than forty-one hours) is higher than among all other people in work. This increase in working hours relates particularly to male

---

17   Shamus Khan, *Privilege: The Making of an Adolescent Elite at St. Paul's School*, Princeton: Princeton University Press, 2010.

18   Savage et al., *Social Class in the Twenty-First Century*, 322–9.

19   Piketty, *Capital in the Twenty-First Century*.

20   John Goldthorpe, 'Social Class Mobility in Modern Britain: Changing Structure, Constant Process', *Journal of the British Academy* 4, 2016, 89–111.

managers in the private sector in the North, few of whom work part-time.

Conversely, in Poland and Romania, such long working hours seem more prevalent among working-class people. This difference in working hours can be explained partly in terms of socio-economic structures: the dominant class in Central and Eastern Europe more often works in small companies or enterprises, where working hours are less codified and regulated. Moreover, in these countries, legal provisions relating to working hours are often less favourable to employees than in the countries of the North and West. Thus the legal working week is forty hours in Hungary, Poland and Romania, compared to thirty-five hours in France and thirty-seven hours in Germany.

The greater satisfaction that managers gain from their work, and the autonomy they enjoy, also help to explain the longer time they spend at work in the North and West of Europe. Half of the members of the dominant class in France, the United Kingdom, Denmark and the Netherlands state that they work days of more than ten hours, whereas the working and middle classes in the countries of the South and the North are usually protected from these hours (but are, on the other hand, more occupied with domestic tasks, especially women). This investment in work manifests the heavy pressure weighing especially on managers in medium and large private-sector enterprises, who are subject to performance targets and requirements for financial profitability. Members of the dominant class in Austria, Denmark, France, the United Kingdom, the Netherlands and Sweden are much more likely than other European people in work to say that they rarely have time to do more than their work, and are subject to 'tight deadlines' for completing their assignments.

Long days and the blurring of boundaries between professional and private life are not limited to managers. As we have already seen, this is also increasingly the fate of many in the intellectual and higher scientific professions, who are subjected to increasing precariousness of work and professional uncertainty, particularly in the cultural industries. This form of intensification of work leads to a particularly high level of commitment, which is manifested in greater investment in professional training. In 2011, 70 per cent of the dominant class in Sweden, 60 per cent in the Netherlands and more than 50 per cent in France and Denmark undertook at least two training courses, paid for either by their employer or by themselves (a language or IT course, management training, etc.), in order to improve their knowledge. The level of such engagement is less than 30 per cent among the dominant class in Bulgaria, Poland, Lithuania and Spain, and falls below 10 per cent in Romania and Greece.

However, this commitment to work among the dominant class in the North and West goes hand in hand with a level of ease at work that other workers do not enjoy. Work that is physically hard, unsocial hours (night work, for example) and exposure to toxic environments remain the attribute of the working class. Executives in the finance industry are even fairly well protected from stress, and contrive to win themselves a high level of autonomy, while at the same time capturing a substantial proportion of the profits.[21] To be specific, members of the dominant class are more able than other workers to choose their hours, to concentrate their work life into fewer days, and to work from home.

Their commitment to work does not at all mean that they retreat from other spheres of social life, such as leisure pursuits, cultural activities and community engagement. The dominant class in the North (especially in the Netherlands, Sweden and Denmark) also has less difficulty in combining work and family life, or taking an hour or two out of their working day to deal with a personal or family problem. These households also have more resources to engage personal-service employees (maids, cleaners, nannies, etc.) or to make use of home delivery services (for example of shopping and meals). In France, managers are seven times more likely than manual workers or unskilled white-collar workers to employ a cleaner. This differentiated relationship with work time and with non-work time redraws the economy of class relations. The social and cultural affluence of the dominant class – that

21   Philippe Askenazy, *Tous rentiers! Pour une autre répartition des richesses*, Paris: Odile Jacob, 2016, 117.

is, their freedom to engage in leisure pursuits or family activities – is determined by the work done for them by the working class, from those working in the food industry to domestic employees.

Thus the commitment of the dominant class of the North and West to work has become a key marker for understanding inequalities in salary and in social standing. Its conditions of work remain much better than those of the working class, despite the fact that some discourses condemning workplace hardship focus eagerly on executive stress and burnout. But, in more global terms, its dominance is no longer justified only in terms of higher educational qualifications and cultural openness: it is also legitimised by an emphasis on prolonged, continuous and intense investment in the professional sphere, to the extent that the workplace now incorporates the personal environment (with sports and leisure facilities, rest spaces, etc.).

This freedom of the dominant class in the North and West has no equivalent in the East. In the former Soviet bloc, the dominant class is highly dependent on the modes of organisation imposed upon it.

### The dominant class of the East: the dominant dominated

The first significant feature of the dominant class in the countries of Central and Eastern Europe is its very recent ascent to its position of dominance. Although some senior apparatchiks of the old bureaucratic and authoritarian regimes managed to convert their capital in order to preserve their positions, the rulers in these societies, which are still in transition, are still quite new and borrow many of their principles from the laws of the market so often trumpeted by the European Union. This situation places the dominant class in the countries of Central and Eastern Europe in a subordinate position vis-à-vis those in the North and West. This subordination not only arises in terms of income, but extends to relations of cultural, political and professional dominance.

Senior managers in these countries experience multiple forms of dependence on those in the countries of the North and West. Many companies established in their countries are headed by European bosses from other countries. In Estonia, for example, the vast majority (80 per cent) of companies that are active outside the country are owned by European shareholders.[22] This subordinate relationship is clearly illustrated by a survey of senior managers in a Romanian bank, which was privatised in the early 2000s and sold to a European multinational.[23] The arrival of a foreign CEO and fifty or so expatriate managers set the Romanian managers at the bank in competition with one another and led to a new organisation of working hours, with much longer working days than during the 1990s. Work time has extended, and is increasingly less distinguishable from personal time. For example, there is a proliferation of team trips and weekend training sessions. This reorganisation allows the senior managers greater autonomy, but also requires them to be more responsible and to exploit themselves, displacing the weight of responsibility from the bank boss to the managers themselves.

Thus managers in Central and Eastern Europe are placed in a subordinate position relative to senior managers in the countries of the North, and this is accompanied by increased professional uncertainty and greater job insecurity. Executive directors and those in the intellectual professions in these countries are more likely than those elsewhere to anticipate the possibility of losing their jobs within six months: among the dominant class, 27 per cent of those in Slovenia and 21 per cent of those in Poland express this fear. This is equivalent to the countries of the South such as Portugal (24 per cent) and Italy (18 per cent), and much higher than the European average of 16 per cent. To be sure, fear for the future also affects the dominant class in countries where job market turnover is high, such as the Netherlands. But in Central and Eastern Europe, this feeling is reinforced by economic structures that are subject to the whims of relocation and the strategies of multinational corporations. In the countries of the

22   Urmas Varblane, Tonu Roolaht, Ele Reiljan and Rein Juriado, 'Estonian Outward Foreign Direct Investments', University of Tartu Economics and Business Administration, working paper 9, 2001.

23   Liviu Chelcea, 'Post-socialist Acceleration: Fantasy Time in a Multinational Bank', *Time and Society* 24: 3, 2015, 348–66.

South, such uncertainty is related more to the austerity policies in place since 2008.

The resources held by the dominant class within each nation, or at least by some within it, are also strongly determined by the dominant class of the North and West. During the years following the fall of the Berlin Wall, privatisation of public enterprises stimulated the buyback of assets by senior managers. The new bosses were, moreover, often engineers or factory directors who had been promoted by the former communist leaders. But their ability to enable these enterprises to survive and prosper depended as much on political support as on their capacity to insert themselves into European and international economic networks.

The policy of promoting managers in one Hungarian gas distribution enterprise that was bought by a large French corporation in the mid-1990s offers a good illustration of this relation of dominance.[24] When the company was privatised, the French directors encouraged the oldest managers to take voluntary redundancy, and replaced them with younger executives drawn from higher social classes. More highly qualified (sometimes educated to master's level) and bilingual, these people are required to demonstrate their willingness to adapt to new forms of management and to move to other countries. Despite their efforts, their careers are relatively limited and their salaries insufficient for them to easily afford a comfortable apartment or readily go on holiday. Nevertheless, through the restructurings, a class of managers acculturated to the values of international competition has come into being. Another example is the case of a manufacturer of baby food in Poland, bought by an American multinational during the 1990s.[25] New administrative, financial and marketing managers with perfect English were recruited and set in competition with

24    Cécile Guillaume and Sophie Pochic, 'Mobilité internationale et carrières des cadres: figure imposée ou pari risqué?', *Formation emploi* 112, 2010, 76–93.

25    Elizabeth C. Dunn, *Privatizing Labor: Baby Food, Big Business and the Remaking of Labor*, Ithaca, NY and London: Cornell University Press, 2004.

older managers deemed 'bureaucratic' and 'inflexible'. These new elect were selected for their aptitude for change, for taking on responsibilities and for imitating the model of the Western manager, even extending to lifestyle and dress.

In the countries of Central and Eastern Europe, educational capital has long been an important resource for winning high social position. But since these countries converted to neoliberalism, the vital importance of qualifications has increased the dependence of elites in the East on the criteria of excellence of the most prestigious Western universities. More than 80 per cent of the dominant class in Poland, Romania, Hungary and Bulgaria have a university degree. But managerial posts are in practice reserved for those with the highest-level qualifications. More than two-thirds of the dominant class in Bulgaria and Poland, and 50 per cent in Hungary, have a master's degree or a doctorate; the proportion is 40 per cent in France and Germany. In the former countries of the East, where the dominant class is smaller and more selective than in the North and West, the high proportion of graduates hides a generational divide between those who went to university before the transition to capitalism and the younger people who received a higher education that is increasingly privately financed.[26] The generation born during the 1960s has found itself prevented from accessing positions of responsibility because they do not have the right qualifications. Many engineers and technical experts trained under the communist regime have found themselves professionally downgraded. On the other hand, women born during the 1950s who have a high level of education have benefited from this process to obtain jobs in the health and education sectors.[27] In Poland, too, the main beneficiaries of the

26   Erzsebet Bukodi and Peter Robert, 'Hungary', in Irena Kogan, Michael Gebel and Clemens Nolke (eds), *Europe Enlarged: A Handbook of Education, Labour and Welfare Regimes in Central and Eastern Europe*, Bristol: The Policy Press, 2008, 183–202.

27   Marie Plessz, 'Des dynamiques générationnelles sexuées: L'accès aux professions très qualifiées pendant la transformation postcommuniste en Hongrie', *Revue française de sociologie* 52: 4, 2011, 657–89.

sharp increase in the number of jobs for managers and engineers during the 2000s have been people under the age of thirty-five.

Responding to the demands of highly skilled jobs arising from the economic transition, the reproduction of the dominant class has been operated through educational capital, alongside new strategies in a context of curriculum diversification. In Hungary, for example, at the time of the massive increase in student numbers during the 1990s, reforms led to a two-tier system within the public universities. At the end of secondary education, school grades and final exam results are converted into points. The highest-achieving students are granted access to university with their tuition fees paid by the state, while students who achieved lower results are also granted university entrance but have to pay for their training themselves, in the absence of a state budget large enough to allow all students to study for free. This system produces sharp social inequalities, since the former, who have enjoyed the most prestigious secondary education, come from families that are more socially endowed than the latter, who are usually of more modest background.

Romania, on the other hand, shifted from an exclusively public university system, which had a little over 160,000 students in 1990, to a higher education system with four times as many students twenty years later, almost half of them in the private sector.[28] In the meantime, the World Bank had become the government's main partner in raising funds for universities, with the aim of training administrators and managers capable of disseminating the precepts of the market economy. The European Community later took up the baton, through a non-refundable grant to finance the introduction and generalisation of management courses. In the space of twenty years, the universities in the former countries of the East have become thriving enterprises serving as a shop window for the entrepreneurial ideology imported from the West.

---

28   Ioana Cîrstocea, 'Les restructurations de l'enseignement supérieur en Roumanie après 1990: Apprentissage international de la gestion, professionnalisation de l'expertise et politisation de l'enjeu universitaire', *Revue d'études comparatives Est-Ouest* 45: 1, 2014, 125–63.

Thus the role of the countries of the North and West of Europe is crucial here too, particularly in the development of a very expensive private sector, for example the International Business School, a training programme set up in Hungary and modelled on the British system. These new courses have been seized on by those members of the dominant class most keen to be part of the conversion to neoliberalism, thus reinforcing the logics of social reproduction already strongly marked in these countries. This process of social reproduction is combined with a professional and academic endogamy more pronounced in Central and Eastern Europe than elsewhere in Europe. Within the dominant class, the essential accumulation of academic capital works to the advantage of managers in the private sector and still more of cultural elites, rather than entrepreneurs. While in 1987 in Poland 32 per cent of university graduates came from intelligentsia families – university lecturers, engineers and senior administrators from before the transition – the rate had reached 51 per cent by 1998, manifesting the ease with which the old-regime managers were able to change track, and their capacity for resisting the new entrepreneurs.[29]

The strategies of differentiation adopted by the dominant class in the East to mark its distinction from the rest of the population are clearly manifested in lifestyle choices, where it keeps its distance from the working class by importing models and lifestyles borrowed from the dominant class of the West. For example, in the major capitals, housing complexes inspired by gated communities have been developed. In Budapest, 240 housing developments were built between 2002 and 2007, with a total of about 37,000 apartments, most of them equipped with twenty-four-hour security systems. Between 1997 and 2007, 200 similar housing developments were constructed in Warsaw.[30] Although these systems are often justified by reference to security considerations in the

29    Tomasz Zarycki, 'Cultural Capital and the Accessibility of Higher Education', *Russian Education and Society* 49: 7, 2007, 41–72.

30    Dominika V. Polanska, 'Gated Communities and the Construction of Social Class Markers in Postsocialist Societies: The Case of Poland', *Space and Culture* 13: 4, 2010, 421–35.

context of weak public institutions, what is really at issue in these residential strategies is the desire of the dominant class to separate itself socially from the working and middle class, who live in tower blocks that were once imposing but are now dilapidated. Young private-sector executives and the intelligentsia pay a great deal of money for their homes in these developments. The social separation is marked spatially by fences, high walls and gates controlled by security staff. Physical enclosure is also a way of privatising the spaces of social and family life.

Outside the capital cities, residential choices are also bound up with the strategies of differentiation that are reconfiguring the social space. In Hungary, new districts of family housing built in the late 1990s and 2000s, on the outskirts of cities such as Dunaújváros, symbolise both a rejection of the built environment of state socialism and an idealisation of Western models of housing for the middle and dominant classes.[31] Unlike gated communities, these districts of detached housing were not created by big property developers, or even by the state. Yet these residences become synonymous with respectability and the distinction of the dominant class. The households that built them previously lived in city-centre apartments, often fashionably decorated and well equipped with the latest technology. While older people are still attached to collective living, younger households value and invest in individual houses. Thus they can avoid both city-centre apartment blocks – even if these are affordable and offer a high level of comfort – and peasant farmers' houses.

Thus housing choice has become a way of manifesting signs of wealth (fine lawns, flower beds and water features, American kitchens and saunas), but also a self-realisation: adornment is used as a marker of financial success and is expressed through aesthetic choices – for example non-rectilinear architectural forms – that break with communist style. This return to the individual private home also goes hand in hand with a valorisation of green spaces entirely opposed to peasant farmers' gardens – greenery now being

---

31   Krisztina Fehérváry, 'The Materiality of the New Family House in Hungary: Postsocialist Fad or Middle Class Ideal?', *City and Society* 23: 1, 2011, 18–41.

associated, as in Western Europe, with well-being and health. This new form of periurban living both redefines and legitimises this emerging class. In the domain of housing, as in that of university course, lifestyles and practices that distinguish the dominant class of Western Europe have been imported into the countries of Central and Eastern Europe, placing local elites under a form of subjection.

Thus the dominant class of Central and Eastern Europe occupies the position of a dominated dominant group: on the one hand it is highly dependent on the dominant class of the North and West for its development, while on the other it adopts strategies and ways of life that consist of permanently differentiating itself from the working and middle classes of its home countries. It is, nevertheless, too early to determine whether this singular form of dependence will persist. From the mid-1990s on, salaries rose much more quickly in the former countries of the East than in the 'West', but the 2008 crisis brought this process to a standstill and it is difficult to say how these gaps might develop.

## CIRCULATION BETWEEN CLASSES AND NATIONS

The treaties on free movement of individuals have markedly stimulated forms of mobility within Europe, with very varying effects in different social groups. On the one hand, company relocations and temporary or permanent migration reinforce the contrasts between Europeans of different social classes and national origins. On the other, the rise in exchanges between countries offers the dominant class multiple opportunities to come into contact with groups that are geographically and socially remote from them. The intensification of these exchanges raises the question whether Europe is a juxtaposition of countries with different lifestyles, or a common space is starting to build, suggesting the emergence of a European society.

*Production and reproduction of class relations through migration*
While national governments have introduced more and more restrictive measures against non-European foreigners, migration within Europe has tended to increase in recent years. Initially

limited to those who had jobs, freedom of movement has now been extended to all European citizens. In total, in 2014, no less than 2.8 million individuals left one of the twenty-eight countries of the EU to settle in another European country.[32] The main destination countries are Germany, the United Kingdom, France and Spain, which is also the country with the highest number of emigrants. Temporary migration is strongly encouraged by European institutions, which consider this kind of mobility a positive phenomenon, in contrast to long-term immigration. Those who leave their country see these displacements as temporary, but as so often in this domain, emigration that was initially for a limited time may end up lasting an entire lifetime. The major metropolises like London, Paris and Brussels are by far the preferred destinations, followed by other cities in the United Kingdom, Sweden, Denmark, Germany and the Netherlands.

The first category of migrants is seasonal workers who head towards centres of employment but maintain links with their region of origin, to the extent that they live in both countries. These intra-European migrants become a sort of invisible population: not being subject to any regulation in terms of entry and length of stay in the destination country, they are rarely officially registered there. Previously, they came mainly from the countries of the South of Europe to work in the North. Today, it is increasingly migrants originating from Central and Eastern Europe who choose to move away to find work, like the women who come to work as nannies, au pairs or cleaners, and the men employed as farm labourers, drivers or manual workers. In the first years after Poland's entry into the European Union in 2004, many millions of workers left the country. In 2007, their main destinations were the United Kingdom (26 per cent) and Ireland (11 per cent). In 2015, Poles represented the largest non-national community in the United Kingdom (16 per cent of migrants), far ahead of Indians (6.9 per cent) and Irish people (6.2 per cent).[33]

---

32   Eurostat, *Migration and Migrant Population Statistics*, 2014.
33   Eurostat, *Migration and Migrant Population Statistics* (2007), 2015.

Freedom of movement within Europe stimulates other migratory flows linked to the service economy and transnational domestic labour. In the countries of the South of Europe such as Italy, where care for children and the elderly was previously provided by the family, it is now entrusted to female workers from the East.[34] Recourse to domestic services has thus increased markedly in Italy and Spain in recent years: women are more likely to be in work, the population is ageing and family structures are changing. In order to meet the needs for childcare and care of the elderly, families call on female migrants from Central and Eastern Europe who come through a rotating system: the domestic help stays in the family for three or four months before her place is taken by a compatriot. Thus a transnational rotation of workers emerges that is organised neither by states nor by employers, but by the migrants themselves. This 'global care chain' is greatly to the advantage of families in the destination countries who have the means to make use of these new domestic services, while families in the countries of origin are those who lose most: they have to manage children and the elderly without the support of those who have chosen to migrate.[35] The migrants themselves are able to supplement their education and return regularly to their country with some savings; for employers, the advantage of these rotating migrations is that they do not spend time and energy finding temporary replacements.

These migrations linked to domestic work represent a clear social fact that tends to bring two axes of the European middle class – those in the country of origin and those in the destination country – into opposition:[36] among the middle class in the West, the employing families are able to access personal services that

34  Sabrina Marchetti, 'Dreaming Circularity? Eastern European Women and Job Sharing in Paid Home Care', *Journal of Immigrant and Refugee Studies* 11: 4, 2013, 347–63.

35  Arlie Russell Hochschild, 'Global Care Chains and Emotional Surplus Value'.

36  Helma Lutz and Ewa Palenga-Möllenbeck, 'Care Workers, Care Drain, and Care Chains: Reflections on Care, Migration, and Citizenship', *Social Politics: International Studies in Gender, State and Society* 19: 1, 2012, 15–37.

were long restricted to the dominant class; for migrants from the East, who often belong to the middle class in their country of origin, this work forms part of a trajectory of mobility and the hope of moving up the social ladder, despite the fact that, in the West, their new career places them among the working class. On both sides, the bulk of duties related to family life rests on women, but the symmetry ends there, for the difference in resources results in very different prospects and solutions: on one side, this domestic labour allows women in the destination countries to reconcile family and work life, while on the other, women from the East have to abandon family in order to meet their needs.

Among the working class in different European countries, the conflicts become apparent through company relocations, which take one of two distinct forms: first, companies moving to countries where labour is cheaper, and second, what can be termed 'on-site' relocations, through the recruitment of newly arrived European immigrants or 'posted' workers. Initially, the opening of borders to employees from the ten new member states in 2004 was conditional on obtaining a work permit. Until 2010, in order to get around these restrictions, many Polish, Romanian and Bulgarian people came to work in France, the Netherlands, Italy and Portugal as self-employed workers. These 'false self-employed workers', taken on at the site and in place of employees by employers looking to minimise their social contributions, were immediately perceived as unfair competition.

At the same time, the application of the 1996 EU Posted Workers' Directive in most European countries constituted a powerful tool for getting around the final restrictions aimed at protecting the countries of the old European Union from these new arrivals. The figure of the posted worker then became the symbol of a threat to preservation of jobs, quality of working conditions and the system of social protection. The wide variations in national minimum wage within the European Union also contributed to increasing and reorienting migrations. The example of the food industry is illuminating in this respect: in 2012, the hourly cost of a posted worker ranged from five euros per hour in Germany to twelve euros per hour in Spain and sixteen euros per hour in France. Thousands of workers from Central and Eastern Europe (Hungary, Romania, Bulgaria) were employed by large German corporations in the meat industry, resulting in the collapse of several French companies which lost their outlets because they were no longer competitive: the closure of the Gad abattoirs in Finistère, with the loss of 900 jobs, is one example. The conflict between the European working class can thus sometimes play out at a distance, when some migrate to deplorable working conditions while others, reproached for costing too much, lose their jobs.

Relocations also had repercussions in countries of emigration. On the national scale, the number of people leaving for more attractive countries may seem relatively small, but at the level of certain regions, migrations for work can look like a haemorrhage of the population. In the Sousa valley in Portugal, migrations to Galicia have decimated an entire region which was already very hard hit by unemployment. From 2003 to 2008, between 90,000 and 120,000 Portuguese workers found work in the construction sector in Spain, while maintaining the possibility of returning home at weekends. Fleeing the crisis in the textile industry and a steep rise in unemployment, most of them arrived as posted workers, with very varied levels of education. Most were only able to obtain precarious contracts that forced them into the role of adjustment variables.[37] Under these conditions, interaction between workers of the two nationalities was reduced to a strict minimum and a mutual mistrust became established between seasonal and local Spanish workers.

In the East, those members of the working class who stayed in their country also saw a change in their situation. From the 1990s onwards, the former state enterprises were systematically dismantled so that local bosses could take over the infrastructure and benefit from the financial support of Western European investors. The aim at that time was to encourage integration into the European Union, but the process continued long after. In Poland, workers

---

37  Bruno Monteiro, 'Portuguese Construction Workers in Spain: Situated Practices and Transnational Connections in the European Field of Construction (2003–2013)', *Construction Labour Review* 2, 2014, 8–32.

habitually contrast enterprises owned by local bosses, where the situation allotted to them is extremely unfavourable and tantamount to exploitation, with those owned by Western European corporations which offer better pay and working conditions. This results in manual and low-skilled workers in these countries coming to feel dependent on Western companies, a situation which, given the collapse of trade unionism, is not without ambivalence: the Western European appears both as a provider of prosperity and as a dominant figure who imposes his/her demands in terms of organisation of labour.

The new potential for movement within the European space thus represents both a threat for some and job prospects for others. Such migration is accompanied by a levelling down of working conditions and a unilateral dissemination of modes of consumption and lifestyles into the countries of emigration.

### The asymmetrical mobility of the dominant class

For the dominant class, by contrast, the opening of the European space to new countries has created a reservoir of possibilities for achieving or improving international careers. But mobility operates differently on either side of the former Iron Curtain.

Senior managers in multinational corporations based in Paris and London, who have accepted or chosen to live in the former countries of the East in order to lead subsidiaries there, see this as a means of gaining autonomy and acquiring the status of CEO.[38] Posted by head office for the purposes of restructuring the organisation of labour and reorganising employees, they find themselves in a local context they know little about, reinforcing the sense of subordination that the elites of the East feel with regard to the countries of the North and West. On the other hand, opportunities for Hungarian or Romanian managers working in subsidiaries of Western European companies to move to France or Germany are less common, and securing them is more difficult and takes longer.

---

38   Cécile Guillaume and Sophie Pochic, 'Mobilité internationale et carrières des cadres: Figure imposée ou pari risqué?', *Formation emploi* 112, 2010, 39–52.

They may even give rise to disappointment when the company does not support relocation of the whole family, which, furthermore, discourages other executives from following the same route.

Migrants who leave of their own accord, with skills that are transferable from one country to another, gain more from moving to the North and West of Europe. Many Polish doctors have taken the opportunity of their country's accession to the European Union to offer their services in the United Kingdom, Sweden and Germany, which offer higher pay and much better working conditions.[39] By contrast, high-skilled women from the East who have migrated by routes other than through their company are less likely to become integrated into the dominant class in the West. Some, qualified as lawyers in their country, find, for example, that their qualification is not sufficient to practise law in Scandinavia.[40] This harsh challenge to their qualifications reveals a restructuring of class relations in Europe, and illustrates the symbolic hierarchy between systems of higher education. Despite these difficulties and obstacles, prolonged contact with countries such as Denmark, which has a wide range of measures aimed at promoting equality at work, encourages these high-skilled women from the East to stay on the labour market, either by making use of their resources as migrants (for example as translators or in professions requiring fluency in two languages) or by returning to studies in the new country to complete their training. In this way, the European space can become, for the few women who manage to find a job at the level of their qualifications, a real opportunity for promotion and a potential route to emancipation.

In some sectors of the economy, such as health, the movement of the dominant class from East to West is not without consequences in the country of emigration. The departure of thousands of Romanian doctors – mostly women who aspire to a better

---

39    Krzysztof Krajewski-Siuda and Piotr Romaniuk, 'Health Worker Emigration from Poland', *Journal of Public Health Policy* 28: 2, 2007, 290–2.

40    Anika Liversage, 'Vital Conjunctures, Shifting Horizons: High-Skilled Female Immigrants Looking for Work', *Work, Employment and Society* 23: 1, 2009, 120–41.

quality of life and improved education and training prospects for their children – to the rich countries of the European Union, including France, has had major effects on the health system and the provision of care in Romania.[41] In leaving their country, doctors leave behind dilapidated hospitals which lack basic medication, to join a French medical system well endowed with modern equipment; in doing so, they thus increase a little further the inequality of care provision between the two countries. The shortage of doctors resulting from these new migrations is partly compensated by the arrival in Romania of doctors from Moldova and the Arab countries, who also hope to be able to continue their migratory journey further West.

In sum, the opening of and subsequent increase in possibilities of moving between West and East form a powerful career accelerator for managers in the private sector in the most economically advanced countries, while for the highest-skilled workers in the East, migration to the richer countries of Europe usually results in downgrading or disillusionment.

## Class relations revealed by relative mobility

Looking beyond the realm of work, the development of the European market does not provide the same resources for all social groups. The opportunities it offers in terms of intra-European mobility are largely determined by class position. Whether it be on the level of university exchanges, relocating in retirement or tourism, there are different forms of mobility that bring Europeans into direct conflict. These individual interactions highlight the inequalities between social classes and between countries, and more generally between the upper and lower levels of the European social space.

For more than a century, exchanges between universities have been a homogenising factor in Europe, but student mobility has increased substantially since it has been supported through

41    Raymonde Séchet and Despina Vasilcu, 'Les migrations de médecins roumains vers la France, entre démographie médicale et quête de meilleures conditions d'exercice', *Norois* 223, 2012, 63–76.

dedicated programmes. When it was set up in 1987, the Erasmus programme offered 3,000 students the opportunity to study in another country; twenty-five years later, in 2012–13, 270,000 students and over 52,000 members of teaching and administrative staff spent time in Europe under this programme.[42] University exchanges between European countries now form an integral part of higher education courses. The United Kingdom, France and Germany are the countries playing host to the largest number of foreign students. But these three countries have all, to varying degrees, instituted mechanisms that favour higher-qualified and better-trained candidates. The United Kingdom, for example, has progressively restricted the number of agreements and partners, by selecting the universities and students capable of meeting the standards of Oxford, which usually boils down to accepting only the most socially advantaged students. This results in a system of selective affinities in which only students already enrolled in prestigious courses can aspire to exchanges with the best European universities. The dominance of the countries of the West and North is also manifested in the restructuring of institutions of higher education. In Poland, for example, a national business school modelled on the French Ecole nationale d'administration (ENA) was set up in 1991. The aim of the Krajowa Szkola Adminstracji Publicznej (National School of Public Administration) is to select the best students and provide them with a generalist training in law, economics and governance in order to provide the Polish state with senior civil servants trained in accordance with Western norms and criteria. Here, too, the rise in exchanges and mobility may well help to bring certain groups closer together, but essentially it becomes an echo chamber, even an amplifier for relations of dominance between countries and social groups.

While young people are those most likely to migrate, there is also a migration of older people, who on retirement, or a little before, choose to move to another European country for reasons of purchasing power, climate or tax advantages. Many pensioners from the major cities in the North leave their home countries to

42   *Erasmus, faits, chiffres et tendances*, European Commission, 2014.

settle in Spain, Portugal and the south of France, the preferred destinations of French, British and German pensioners. In Tocina, a town in the east of the Costa del Sol, many services have been developed in response to the needs of British pensioners: pubs, fish and chip restaurants and bookshops selling English-language books and magazines have appeared in this Spanish setting.[43] In becoming expatriates, these pensioners have the sense of living a second life; they do not necessarily seek to integrate with the local population, but redefine themselves in contact with the Belgians and Germans who have come, like them, to find a new social life in a better environment.

Finally, tourism within Europe is another form of mobility that can increase interaction between populations by enabling them to discover the cultures and lifestyles of other Europeans. Increasing numbers of people take holidays within Europe, and these forms of seasonal relocation also contribute to changing class relations in the cities most involved. In some countries, tourism makes a major economic contribution to the national wealth, even if the local people rarely go on holiday. Greece offers a telling example: 'cultural enterprises' form as large a proportion of the tertiary sector overall as in the Nordic countries, but the level of cultural participation of Greek people is the lowest in Europe. Thus the presence of producers of cultural goods, particularly through tourism, does not necessarily imply cultural engagement on the part of those living in the country, but may constitute a factor attracting other Europeans. When the phenomenon takes off, some city centres effectively become open-air museums, moving local residents to the distant margins and transforming the cityscape into a tourist spectacle.

Those who travel most are aged between twenty-five and thirty-nine, and are generally among the most highly educated. In 2012, 85 per cent of foreign trips made by European residents were to another country in Europe, and the main means of transport

---

43   Caroline Olivier, 'Imagined Communitas: Older Migrants and Aspirational Mobility', in Vered Amit (ed.), *Going First Class? New Approaches to Privileged Travel and Movement*, New York: Berghahn Books, 2007, 126–43.

was long-distance coach.[44] In some countries, holidays within national boundaries make up the majority of trips (95 per cent in Romania, 92 per cent in Spain and Greece, 90 per cent in Portugal, 89 per cent in France), while in others, such as Belgium and Switzerland, more than half of all travel is to another European country. In most cases, tourism is to neighbouring countries, but some countries are more highly valued than others, including Spain (the preferred destination for eleven countries), Germany (for nine countries), Italy (for nine countries), France (for eight countries) and Croatia (for four countries). Some cities in Central and Eastern Europe are gradually becoming holiday destinations and are attempting in this way to rebuild their economic significance – with sometimes mixed results: in their interactions with tourists, the residents of Varna try to offer an image of the Bulgarian nation turned towards the future, defining themselves as cosmopolitan and welcoming.[45] But the tourists reflect back the image of Bulgaria as a poor nation confined to the margins of Europe or even belonging to the Third World.

All of these forms of mobility and migration contribute to permanently reshaping class relations within the European space. Socialised through both their class background and their nationality, migrants have a direct and brutal experience of the relations of power that play out between Europeans, depending on their social position and country of origin.

The European Union guarantees a space of free movement which appears to be the same for all, but in reality reproduces, and even deepens, inequalities. The opportunities offered by intra-European mobility are more accessible to the dominant and middle class than to the working class, particularly for those in the North of Europe. For the groups with the greatest financial and social resources, European integration without harmonisation of social rights allows them, for example, to travel to and access goods in the countries of the East and South at prices lower than in the North,

44   Eurostat, news releases, 27 June 2014.
45   Carla Bethmann, 'Clean, Friendly, Profitable?': Tourism and the Tourism Industry in Varna, Bulgaria, Zurich and Berlin: Lit, 2014.

since labour is cheaper there. The dominant and middle class of the North thus accumulate linguistic resources, social capital that can be monetised on the labour market, and low-cost activities and services (skiing in Bansko or enjoying spa holidays in Varna in Bulgaria).

Measuring the economic and social effects of European policies necessitates going beyond a country-by-country reading: power relations do not stay strictly within national boundaries, and are reshaped by the shifts in capitalism, the policies of individual states and the European Union directives that go alongside them. Whether through migration for work, for education, for tourism or more indirectly through transfers of economic activity or orders issued by managers in head offices to the subsidiaries of large European corporations, relations between social groups are being permanently redefined on a European-wide scale. To be sure, social groups are still strongly determined within nations, but the international division of labour between European countries is reformulating and altering the balance of the inequalities running through them on the regional level. Moreover, the national foundation of social groups is continually being disrupted by migrations and the European legislative framework; differences between countries generate relations of dominance between classes, whether near at hand or at a distance, on the European level and beyond national boundaries. The Europeanisation of trade and of political and academic institutions works to the advantage of the dominant class, who are thus able to accumulate cultural, academic, linguistic and financial resources by internationalising themselves, and hence to expand their power. By contrast, European construction as it has operated for the last several decades is much less to the advantage of the working class: those in the countries worst hit by restructuring are forced to leave their country for work, while others are threatened by the relocation of their companies. The effects of neoliberal reform are very different depending on whether they are viewed from the top or the bottom of the social hierarchy. This results in class antagonisms that regularly resurface during European Union elections.

# 5

# Are Classes Mobilised at the European Level?

Our description of the European social space in the preceding chapters has identified the characteristics of social classes in Europe, their common features, their differences and their relations across national boundaries. But do these 'classes on paper' translate into 'mobilised classes'?[1] If there is a 'globalised hyper-bourgeoisie' mobilised in defence of its interests at the European level,[2] the same cannot be said for the working and middle classes, who show none of the obvious signs of a class conscious of its own interests. Although its members form the majority of the population, the working class remains marginalised and is invisible within European political institutions that present themselves as representative. Nor do they have any identified representative body that could serve as a rallying point at this level. Does this mean that there is no class opposition in the European arena? Surely not: conflicts around pay, working conditions and forms of social welfare abound, and increasingly extend beyond national boundaries. Nevertheless, those involved in these struggles do not have the sense of belonging to a social class, and find it difficult to imagine coming together or even coming to an understanding with social groups who share their concerns but live in other countries.

1   Pierre Bourdieu, 'What Makes a Social Class? On the Theoretical and Practical Existence of Groups', *Berkeley Journal of Sociology* 32, 1987, 1–17.
2   Bruno Cousin and Sebastien Chauvin, 'Globalizing Forms of Elite Sociability: Varieties of Cosmopolitanism in Paris Social Clubs', *Ethnic and Racial Studies* 37: 12, 2014, 2209–25.

In his account of the making of the English working class, E. P. Thompson stressed that this class was consolidated in adversity; that is, in reaction to the decline in ways of life and the destruction of popular cultures caused by the development of industrial capitalism.[3] Subjected to increasingly intense economic exploitation and to political oppression, the British workers of the late eighteenth century became aware of their shared interests, uniting amongst themselves against the industrial bourgeoisie. Thompson also highlights the importance of institutions such as friendly societies, which enabled the workers to protect themselves collectively against the harsh living conditions under this new economic regime. The shared experience of pauperisation fostered the emergence of a collective consciousness, and made self-organisation essential. Cycles of social mobilisation and repression were also major factors in the formation of a relatively unified class. This analysis raises the question whether the class antagonisms that exist in twenty-first-century Europe could lead to a similar process of class consolidation. In Bourdieu's view, the shift from a class 'on paper' to a mobilised class is necessarily the product of symbolic struggles that aim to impose the legitimacy of a particular social group in the domain of collective representation. In this context, intellectuals, activists in trade unions and political organisations play a decisive role. It is, then, worth asking whether the conditions of possibility exist for such a collective work of representation and symbolic unification of the European working class.

This approach invites us once again to go beyond purely national divisions, and not to limit the question of the future of the European Union to an argument over the functioning of institutions. The traditional left/right cleavage seems to be more and more obsolete and tends to be supplanted by the construction of a 'bourgeois bloc' gathering the skilled and affluent pro-EU social groups.[4] The issue is, then, to explore the conditions under which the working and

---

3   E. P. Thompson, *The Making of the English Working Class*, London: Gollancz, 1963.

4   Bruno Amable and Stefano Palombarini, 'The Bloc Bourgeois in France and Italy', in Hideko Magara (eds), *Economic Crises and Policy Regimes*, Edward Elgar Publishing, Northampton, MA, 2014, 177–216.

middle classes might take political action and articulate demands in such a way as to overturn the existing balance of power.

## CLASS IN CONFLICT IN AND WITH THE EUROPEAN UNION

From its inception, the European Community has been the domain of economic, administrative and intellectual elites who, defeated at the end of the Second World War, sought to re-establish themselves and to promote a single market.[5] Since then, Europe has been constructed as a zone of free exchange fostering the free flow of capital, competition and competitiveness. Over the years a security dimension has been added, focused on controlling migratory flows and subsequently on the fight against terrorism, but the promise of a European social policy has always been postponed until later, and in the end is yet to arrive.[6]

*The dominant class's interest in the European political project*
The economic elites have benefited from the liberalisation of the European labour market and have gained more openings for investment.[7] By maintaining the fight against inflation as its top priority, the European Central Bank favours the owners of financial assets, and by privileging the free flow of capital, it allows large corporations to set their sites of production in competition with one another. Similarly, the European Commission's policy decisions on the regulation of economic markets and on grants to enterprises benefit the directors and managers of large companies, to the detriment of those in medium and small enterprises who do not have the resources to influence European institutions.[8]

---

5   Wolfgang Streeck, *Buying Time: The Delayed Crisis of Democratic Capitalism*, London: Verso Books, 2014.
6   François Denord and Antoine Schwartz, *L'Europe sociale n'aura pas lieu*, Paris: Raisons d'agir, 2009, 119.
7   Matthew Gabel and Harvey D. Palmer, 'Understanding Variation in Public Support for European Integration'. *European Journal of Political Research* 27: 1, 1997, 3–19.
8   Sylvain Laurens, *Lobbyists and Bureaucrats in Brussels: Capitalism's Brokers*, London: Routledge, 2017.

There is a central kernel of the dominant class that is highly socialised in the ways of Europe, its codes and practices: senior civil servants, lobbyists, members of the European Parliament, commissioners, experts and some entrepreneurs.[9] These dominant sections of the dominant class have taken full advantage of the possibilities of mobility within Europe, thus reinforcing their social and political cohesion.[10] By contrast, the working and middle classes in general have benefited much less from these developments; the migration of some workers from the East and South of Europe has even been perceived by people in the North and West as a new form of competition rather than a desirable cohesion.

Other sections of the dominant class are less well placed to take advantage of European Union policy, but still find compensations there. For example, university teachers and researchers have suffered under budgetary adjustment policies imposed by Brussels and the norms of New Public Management in European universities,[11] but some of them have benefited considerably from the substantial funding that was offered them – grants from the European Research Council, European research and exchange programmes, etc. More broadly, policies in the domain of higher education and research support the circulation of these intellectuals, who in response form their own organisations (consortia, associations) to represent their interests to the European Commission. The same is true for artists, football club managers and lawyers, who have played the role of intermediaries between the various sections of the elite involved in the construction of the European Union.[12] The dominant class's interest in Europe is manifested in

9   Didier Georgakakis (ed.), *Le champ de l'eurocratie: Une sociologie politique du personnel de l'UE*, Paris: Economica, 2012.

10   Ettore Recchi and Adrian Favell (eds), *Pioneers of European Integration: Citizenship and Mobility in the EU*, Cheltenham: Edward Elgar Publishing, 2009.

11   Chris Lorenz, 'If You're So Smart, Why Are You under Surveillance? Universities, Neoliberalism, and New Public Management', *Critical Inquiry* 38: 3, 2012, 599–629.

12   Schotté Manuel, 'La structuration du football professionnel européen: Les fondements sociaux de la prévalence de la "spécificité sportive",

elections: support for Europe is higher among managers than among manual workers and unemployed people, higher among graduates than among those whose studies were limited, and higher among city dwellers than among those living in rural areas.[13]

The political and economic orientations adopted by the European Union have helped to establish a multi-tiered Europe that works mainly to the advantage of the dominant class, or rather one part of it, while other social groups remain untouched by these benefits.[14]

## A politics that works against the working class

By creating its own single currency, an independent central bank and membership criteria that apply to all countries, the EU has eliminated the tools that nation states had at their disposal for regulating their economy: exchange policy (via devaluation) and budgetary policy (via public investment and company tax policy). The cost of labour has thus become the last remaining adjustment variable for national economies, and this has played strongly to the disadvantage of the working class.

This tendency was aggravated by the 2008 crisis. The choice to pursue a policy of austerity and of massive public support for private banks has resulted in a drastic fall in tax revenues. This has penalised the working class in European countries, partly because they are more at risk of unemployment, and partly because they are more dependent on social benefits, which have been sharply cut in order to meet the restrictive criteria for budget deficits. In 2014, more than 115 million Europeans were at risk of poverty or social exclusion.[15] The encouragement to liberalise labour markets in Europe has destabilised the conditions of employment of the

*Revue française de socio-économie* 13: 1, 2014, 85–106. Antoine Vauchez, 'Une élite d'intermédiaires: Genèse d'un capital juridique européen (1950–1970)', *Actes de la recherche en sciences sociales* 166–7, 2007, 54–65.

13  Hanspeter Kriesi, Edgar Grande, Martin Dolezal, Marc Helbling, Dominic Höglinger, Swen Hutter and Bruno Wüest, *Political Conflict in Western Europe*, Cambridge: Cambridge University Press, 2012.

14  Etienne Balibar, *We, the People of Europe? Reflections on Transnational Citizenship*. Princeton: Princeton University Press, 2004.

15  Eurostat, Press release 155/2017, 16 October 2017.

working class (cf. Chapter 1). Whether it be directives on the working hours of lorry drivers or on posted workers, the policies pursued by European leaders in relation to social law and public services very often have the effect of challenging protective standards created at national level. The European Union is thus fostering the breakdown of national support structures without developing new forms of protection to replace them.

In the domain of agriculture, subsidies distributed under the Common Agricultural Policy (CAP) have favoured the amalgamation and modernisation of farms, to the detriment of the smallest. In Central and Eastern Europe, in the years between 2003 and 2007, the agricultural labour force diminished twice as rapidly as in the rest of the European Union. Thanks to the subsidies, the largest farms were able to specialise in major crops, but small family farms were greatly weakened, forcing them to let go of workers employed there.[16] For a long time, however, Poland remained an exception to this rule, both in that the proportion of agricultural workers fell less than elsewhere and because small farms still represent a refuge from economic restructuring. Since the 2008 crisis, the policy of support for the poorest regions of Europe has been scaled back, and its very existence challenged – one further step in the abandonment of the working class.[17] Thus the social Europe so often proclaimed by European leaders since the Treaty of Rome in 1957 remains a dead letter.

How long can such a neoliberal policy last? While national governments are subject to the sanctions of universal suffrage, European leaders give the impression of being immovable, or at least beyond the reach of rejection by the electorate. This stability is partly due to the fact that Europe lacks any space of political deliberation in which a change in the rules for decision-making could be demanded.[18] Decision-making bodies such as the European Commission,

16   Nigel Swain, 'Agriculture "East of the Elbe" and the Common Agricultural Policy', *Sociologia Ruralis* 53: 3, 2013, 369–89.

17   Streeck, *Buying Time*.

18   Jürgen Habermas, *The Structural Transformation of the Public Sphere: An Inquiry into a Category of Bourgeois Society* (1962), Cambridge, MA: MIT Press, 1989.

the European Central Bank and even the European Parliament keep their distance from the people of Europe, thus giving credence to the conviction that it is difficult, perhaps impossible, to make changes in this institutional space that would lead to social progress. The entire history of the construction of Europe was achieved through institutions remote from the people, around bureaucratic structures that exist independently of European society.[19]

Despite this exclusion, the issue of Europe has become politicised, a fact manifested, in referendums, by a collapse in trust in the European Union.[20] Today, splits over Europe are played out in every national election, disrupting the traditional debates between left and right and connecting back to class antagonisms.

## CLASS ANTAGONISM CONTAINED WITHIN NATIONAL BORDERS

Far from being absent from the concerns of the working class, Europe is becoming a key issue in every election. But the peculiar feature of these new class conflicts is that they are not located in a European arena of mobilisation: they remain confined within national boundaries.

### The working class's distance from and opposition to the European Union

Class conflicts are expressed at European level primarily through elections: every election points to the growing rejection of the European Union's economic policies.

While the members of the European working class may not have a clear vision of all the decisions taken by the European Union,[21] they

---

19   Hartmut Kaelble, *A Social History of Europe, 1945–2000: Recovery and Transformation after Two World Wars*, New York: Berghahn Books, 2013.

20   Sara B. Hobolt and James Tilley, *Blaming Europe? Responsibility without Accountability in the European Union*, Oxford: Oxford University Press, 2014.

21   In 2013, only 52 per cent of Europeans knew that members of the European Parliament are elected directly by the citizens of each member state. European Commission, *Public Opinion in the European Union*, July 2013, 14.

are aware of the risks its economic orientations create for the future of their work. Their political and symbolic distance from projects pursued by Brussels is manifested first in elections to the European Parliament. Between the 1980s and 2014, average turnout in European elections has fallen consistently, moving from 58 per cent in 1989 to 50 per cent in 1999, before dropping to 43 per cent in 2009 and 2014.[22] This very low turnout is particularly pronounced in the countries of the East: it is below 40 per cent in Romania, Hungary, Poland, Latvia, Bulgaria, Estonia, the Czech Republic, Slovakia and Slovenia. In these countries, the level of involvement in community organisations, trade unions and political parties is lower than everywhere else in Europe, owing to an enduring mistrust in forms of engagement that were previously compulsory.[23] Moreover, since it was the elites who led the process of these countries joining the European Union, a large proportion of the middle and working classes has remained indifferent to it, and more sensitive to domestic problems.[24] Two decades after the first gestures of rapprochement with Europe, right-wing parties have been converted to Euroscepticism, and left-wing parties find themselves trapped by the contrast between the high expectations raised by social Europe and the general failure to meet them. When Hungary entered the European Union, the majority of Hungarians (63 per cent) stated that they thought that joining the EU would be a good thing for their country; one year later only 49 per cent expressed this view. The same sense of disappointment was expressed in Poland (from 61 to 50 per cent).[25]

Participation in European elections has also fallen in several countries of the South. While in the late 1990s it was above 50 per

22  Data from the European Parliament.

23  Marc Morjé Howard, *The Weakness of Civil Society in Post-Communist Europe*. Cambridge: Cambridge University Press, 2003.

24  Attila Agh, 'The Hungarian Left and the European Integration Process: The Bitter-Sweet Success of Return to Europe', in Michael Holmes and Knut Roder, *The Left and the European Constitution: From Laeken to Lisbon*, Manchester: Manchester University Press, 2012, 224.

25  Laure Neumayer, 'Les opinions publiques en Europe centrale sur l'Union européenne, avant et après l'adhésion', *Le courrier des pays de l'est* 1048: 2, 2005, 74–87.

cent in Spain and Portugal, turnout is now at the same level as in the East. There has also been a substantial drop in turnout in founding countries of the EU such as France and Germany, where it is now below 50 per cent. Turnout was above 50 per cent in only six countries in the last elections in 2014 (including Belgium, Luxembourg, Denmark and Greece, where voting is compulsory). Thus the election of representatives to its Parliament is a matter of indifference.

*Table 14. Rate of Participation in Elections to the European Parliament since 1979, by Country (%)*

| Country | 1979 | 1984 | 1989 | 1994 | 1999 | 2004 | 2009 | 2014 | 2019 |
|---|---|---|---|---|---|---|---|---|---|
| Belgium | 91 | 92 | 91 | 91 | 91 | 91 | 90 | 90 | 88 |
| Denmark | 48 | 52 | 46 | 53 | 50 | 48 | 60 | 56 | 66 |
| Germany | 66 | 57 | 62 | 60 | 45 | 43 | 43 | 48 | 61 |
| Ireland | 64 | 48 | 68 | 44 | 50 | 59 | 59 | 52 | 50 |
| France | 61 | 57 | 49 | 53 | 47 | 43 | 41 | 42 | 50 |
| Italy | 86 | 82 | 81 | 74 | 70 | 72 | 65 | 57 | 54 |
| Luxembourg | 89 | 89 | 87 | 89 | 87 | 91 | 91 | 86 | 84 |
| Netherlands | 58 | 51 | 47 | 36 | 30 | 39 | 37 | 37 | 42 |
| United Kingdom | 32 | 32 | 36 | 36 | 24 | 39 | 35 | 36 | 37 |
| Greece | 81 (1981) | 81 | 80 | 73 | 70 | 63 | 53 | 60 | 59 |
| Spain | | | 55 | 59 | 63 | 45 | 45 | 44 | 61 |
| Portugal | | | 51 | 36 | 40 | 39 | 37 | 34 | 31 |
| Sweden | | | | 42 (1995) | 39 | 38 | 46 | 51 | 55 |
| Austria | | | | 68 (1996) | 49 | 42 | 46 | 45 | 60 |
| Finland | | | | 58 (1996) | 30 | 39 | 39 | 39 | 41 |
| Czech Republic | | | | | | 28 | 28 | 18 | 29 |
| Estonia | | | | | | 27 | 44 | 37 | 38 |

| | | | | | | | | | |
|---|---|---|---|---|---|---|---|---|---|
| Cyprus | | | | | | 73 | 59 | 44 | 45 |
| Lithuania | | | | | | 48 | 21 | 47 | 53 |
| Latvia | | | | | | 41 | 54 | 30 | 34 |
| Hungary | | | | | | 39 | 36 | 29 | 43 |
| Malta | | | | | | 82 | 79 | 75 | 73 |
| Poland | | | | | | 21 | 25 | 24 | 46 |
| Slovenia | | | | | | 28 | 28 | 25 | 29 |
| Slovakia | | | | | | 17 | 20 | 13 | 23 |
| Bulgaria | | | | | | 29 (2007) | 39 | 36 | 33 |
| Romania | | | | | | 29 (2007) | 28 | 32 | 51 |
| Croatia | | | | | | | | 25 | 30 |
| European Union | 62 | 59 | 58 | 57 | 50 | 45 | 43 | 43 | 51 |

*Source*: European Parliament.

This abstention defines a boundary between the upper and lower levels of the social hierarchy, whatever the indicator used to evaluate it. In 2014, manual workers and unemployed people were more likely to abstain,[26] as were those with the lowest qualifications and the least wealthy.[27] Thus a large proportion of the working class refuses to declare an opinion in elections to the European Parliament.

However, the last elections in 2019 marked a resurgence of voter turnout (51 per cent, + 8 percentage points). While voter

26   Nonna Mayer, Allison Rovny, Jan Rovny and Nicolas Sauger, 'Outsiderness, Social Class, and Votes in the 2014 European Elections', *Revue européenne des sciences sociales* 53: 1, 2015, 157–76.

27   André Blais and Filip Kostelka, 'The Decision to Vote or Abstain in the 2014 European Elections', *Revue européenne des sciences sociales* 53: 1, 2015, 79–94. Nicholas Clark, 'Explaining Low Turnout in European Elections: The Role of Issue Salience and Institutional Perceptions in Elections to the European Parliament', *Journal of European Integration* 36: 4, 2014, 339–56.

turnout remained stable or even declined in some countries (Ireland, Italy, Portugal, Greece, Cyprus, Estonia, Bulgaria, Sweden and Great Britain), it rose sharply (+ 10 percentage points) in Hungary, Romania, Poland, the Czech Republic, Austria, Spain, Germany and Denmark. Despite this increase in electoral turnout, the abstention rate remained above 50 per cent in Eastern European countries. According to the Eurobarometer post-election survey,[28] while the increase in voter turnout compared to 2014 affected all social groups, it is higher among managers (+ 8 percentage points, 61 per cent) and white-collar workers (+ 9 percentage points, 53 per cent) than among manual workers (+ 7 percentage points, 42 per cent) and the unemployed (+ 6 percentage points, 37 per cent). It is particularly important among students (+ 14 percentage points, 51 per cent). As a result, social inequalities in participation increased during this election.

Several explanatory factors may have influenced the increase in voter turnout. However, it seems that the polarisation of the issues on the future of Europe and the importance given to climate change have been decisive. In this context, the classic parties of the right and left tended to lose ground in favour of the far right (France, Italy, Great Britain, Germany, Sweden) or nationalist right (Poland, Hungary) on the one hand, and to the Greens (Germany, France, Belgium, Luxembourg, Finland, Ireland) on the other. According to the Eurobarometer survey, in the richest European countries, the main issue of the elections was concern for the climate and environmental protection, while in the poorer it was about economic growth.

While few are motivated to vote in European elections, electoral consultations on the programme of the European Union generate much higher levels of participation and more animated debate, particularly in the countries of the North. The 2005 referendum in France on the European constitution, and the 2016 referendum in the United Kingdom on leaving the EU, are particularly telling examples of this high level of mobilisation of the electorate, leading to a rejection of European Union

---

28 European Parliament, *Eurobarometer: Post-election Survey 2019. First Results*, June 2019.

institutions. In both cases, the issue was not the single currency, but the relationship with European institutions and their policies. In France, the turnout in the referendum on the European constitution was especially high (69 per cent), compared to the very low turnout a year earlier for the European elections (43 per cent). While turnout among manual workers always lags well behind that among senior managers, this was not the case when the issue was agreement with the European constitution, which was rejected by 54.4 per cent of French people. Whatever method we choose (opinion polls or geographical analysis), it is clear that the majority of the working class was opposed to the constitutional treaty, while the majority of the dominant class voted for it. Between two-thirds and four-fifths of manual workers, and around 60 per cent of unskilled white-collar workers, voted no, compared to only a third of senior managers.[29] Similarly, among middle-class employees the great majority of public-sector workers voted against the treaty. Between 1992 and 2005, rejection of European institutions grew primarily among the working and middle classes.

Over ten years later, the referendum in the United Kingdom on whether to leave or stay in the European Union was set in a different context, but also reflects class antagonisms that are a little too readily forgotten.[30] While for many years the working class had withdrawn into abstention in national and European elections, its participation unexpectedly rose in the referendum, to 72.2 per cent compared to 66 per cent in the 2015 general election.[31] Many commentators interpreted this electoral episode in terms of a series of oppositions – globalisation's winners against its losers, citizens open to immigration and international cooperation versus those opposed to them

---

29   Patrick Lehingue, 'Le Non français au traité constitutionnel européen (mai 2005): Sur deux lectures "polaires" du scrutin', *Actes de la recherche en sciences sociales* 166–7, 2007, 123–39.

30   Sascha Becker, Thiemo Fetzer and Dennis Novy, 'Who Voted for Brexit? A Comprehensive District-Level Analysis', *Economic Policy* 92: 32, 2017, 601–50.

31   Geoffrey Evans, 'Postscript: Brexit as an Expression of the "Democratic Class Struggle"', in Geoffrey Evans and James Tilley, *The New Politics of Class: The Political Exclusion of the British Working Class*, Oxford: Oxford University Press, 2017, 201–8.

– whereas in reality the debate revealed class divisions: 57 per cent of senior managers and professionals voted to stay in the EU, while 64 per cent of skilled manual workers, low-skilled white-collar workers and unskilled manual workers voted to leave.[32] Rather than being purely the expression of anti-immigrant feeling, the vote for Brexit chosen by 52 per cent of the electorate extended well beyond UKIP supporters, who were primarily drawn from the lower middle class (self-employed workers and small business owners).[33] British voters' rejection of the EU may also be understood as a criticism of the economic policies pursued by the European Union.

This rejection by the working class is also observed in the 2012 referendum in Ireland on the European Stability and Growth Pact. A few years earlier, political debates in France around the European constitution had already demonstrated that the Euroscepticism of the working class and trade unions was related more to a rejection of European policies than to a cultural attachment to their nation.[34]

This class antagonism, which regularly emerges in European elections and is systematically glossed over by politicians who prefer to talk of 'populism' or 'Euroscepticism',[35] is not manifested in the same way everywhere in Europe. In the 2015 referendum in Greece on adoption of the first memorandum,[36] which was

32  See lordashcroftpolls.com. See also, using a different classification of social position, Tak Wing Chan, Morag Henderson, Maria Sironi and Juta Kawalerowicz, 'Understanding the Social and Cultural Bases of Brexit', UCL working paper, 2017.

33  Geoffrey Evans and Jon Mellon, 'Working Class Votes and Conservative Losses: Solving the UKIP Puzzle', *Parliamentary Affairs* 69: 2, 2016, 464–79.

34  Elodie Béthoux, Roland Erne and Darragh Golden, 'A Primordial Attachment to the Nation? French and Irish Workers and Trade Unions in Past EU Referendum Debates', *British Journal of Industrial Relations* 56: 3, 2018, 656–78.

35  Sarah Hobolt and Catherine E. de Vries, 'Turning against the Union? The Impact of the Crisis on the Eurosceptic Vote in the 2014 European Parliament Elections', *Electoral Studies* 44, 2016, 504–14.

36  The First Economic Adjustment Programme for Greece, a proposed agreement between the Greek government and the EU, the ECB and the IMF, to finance the country's debt in exchange for a series of austerity measures and privatisation of the Greek economy.

rejected by 61 per cent of voters, the main opposition came from young people, who suffered most from austerity policies, and from pensioners who, attached to their savings, feared that Greece might leave the eurozone. But it also pitted doctors, lawyers and engineers (the majority of whom voted for the memorandum) against the unemployed (72 per cent of whom voted no) and the very broad category of private-sector employees (73 per cent of whom voted no). In the Athens region the vote was clearly determined by the class structure in districts and boroughs:[37] in the areas with the most developed tourism industry and the largest farms – subsidised by the EU – opposition to the memorandum was lower.

These European referendums reveal the importance of class divisions. The resistance of the middle and working classes is not a rejection of all European projects, but a refusal of the neoliberal policies being pursued. Their main concern is to preserve certain protections, against the challenge to national social entitlements, but this demand takes different forms in different countries.

*European social expectations varying from country to country*

According to Eurobarometer polls, the majority of Europeans today are in favour of standardisation of social-welfare systems (64 per cent in 2017, 62 per cent in 2006), but there are significant variations between countries.[38] On the one hand, the vast majority of those living in the East and South of Europe are in favour of standardisation of social welfare: 86 per cent of Hungarians and 69 per cent of Italians support it. On the other, people in Scandinavia, the United Kingdom, Germany, the Netherlands, Austria and France are less keen on the idea.

In another European survey (European Social Survey), on the question whether people are in favour of or opposed to a system of

---

37   Kostas Rontos, Efstathios Grigoriadis, Adele Sateriano, Maria Syrmali, Ioannis Vavouras and Luca Salvati, 'Lost in Protest, Found in Segregation: Divided Cities in the Light of the 2015 "Οχι" Referendum in Greece', *City, Culture and Society* 7: 3, 2016, 139–48.

38   Eurobarometer, Special Eurobarometer 467 – Wave EB88.1 – TNS opinion and social.

social protections common across the European Union, the middle class in the public sector (teachers, health associate professionals, legal and social associate professionals) and employees and skilled workers among the working class (receptionists and customer service clerks, skilled manual workers, drivers) are more supportive of social Europe. According to the same survey, 42 per cent of Europeans think that the services provided as social welfare in their country would be 'lower if more decisions were taken by the European Union', 28 per cent think that their social entitlements would be similar, and only 23 per cent think that they would be higher. Beneath these average figures, there is a strong contrast between people in the countries of the East (Estonia, Poland, Slovenia, Czech Republic), more of whom (between 40 and 53 per cent) believe that social benefits and services provided in their country would be 'greater if more decisions were taken by the European Union'. In countries like France, Ireland, Germany, the Netherlands and Sweden, the European Union is viewed more as a neoliberal institution that would reduce social entitlements, and this view seems to be shared by all social classes. These opinions are relevant when we consider the inequalities in social protection in Europe. While on average EU countries spend 28 per cent of their GDP on social benefits, it falls to less than 20 per cent in Eastern Europe.[39] In addition, the per capita gaps are high: the average amount of social benefits is about €10,000 per year (in purchasing-power standard) for a French and a German, around €5,000 for a Portuguese or a Greek, €4,000 for a Hungarian or a Pole and €2,500 for a Romanian. Thus the protection of old age or sickness remains unequal and, in some countries of Europe, households are responsible for healthcare. While in France health expenditure paid directly by households is less than 10 per cent of overall health expenditure, it is 35 per cent in Greece, 30 per cent in Hungary and 25 per cent in Spain. More than on any other continents, especially the United States, the working class in Europe has been built on the achievement of high levels of social rights and social protection. The construction of the European

---

39   Eurostat data, Sespros, 2015.

Union, which puts social-protection systems in competition with one another, encourages divisions within the working classes in Europe, particularly between those in the North and the West who fear a downward levelling of social rights and those in the East who are disappointed not to see the promise of progress on this issue materialise.

National social-welfare systems have been seriously eroded by EU injunctions to reduce public spending, but have not been replaced or supplemented by forms of social security shared across countries. The national structure therefore remains a system providing protection for the working class, who generally continue to see the institutions of the European Union as impervious to social demands. For the working class of the North and West, the European Union represents a threat, which they reject through their votes. For the working class in the South and East, the issue is rather that of promised new benefits that are now also being cast into doubt. Even so, these resistances have up to now not been sufficient to generate class mobilisation at European level.

*The shortcomings of European studies on*
*social opinions and expectations*
The few quantitative studies measuring Europeans' expectations in terms of social entitlements are based on a series of assumptions that orient questions in such a way as to produce interpretations in terms of national divisions.

Eurobarometer 2017 covers all the countries of the European Union (EU 28, n = 27,881). Respondents are asked their opinions on the standardisation of social-welfare systems within the European Union, through the following questions:

1. For each of the following areas, please tell me if you believe that more decision-making should take place at a European level or, on the contrary, that less decision-making should take place at a European level:

Dealing with health and social-security issues
More decision-making at a European level
Less decision-making at a European level
No change is needed (SPONTANEOUS)

2. Today, each European Union Member State is responsible for its own social-welfare system. To what extent would you be in favour or opposed to the harmonisation of social-welfare systems within the European Union?

Strongly in favour
Somewhat in favour
Somewhat opposed
Strongly opposed

The European Social Survey 2016 was conducted in thirteen EU countries (with 13,218 people in work), and asks respondents their views on a proposed European social protection:

'It has been proposed that there should be a European Union-wide social benefit scheme for all poor people. In a moment I will ask you to tell me whether you are against or in favour of this scheme. First, look at the highlighted box at the top of this card, which shows the main features of the scheme. A European Union-wide social-benefit scheme includes all of the following: . . . READ OUT . . .

The purpose is to guarantee a minimum standard of living for all poor people in the European Union.
The level of social benefit people receive will be adjusted to reflect the cost of living in their country.'

The scheme would require richer European Union countries to pay more into such a scheme than poorer European Union countries.
INTERVIEWER: PAUSE TO GIVE THE RESPONDENT TIME TO READ CARD.

> Overall, would you be against or in favour of having such a European Union-wide social benefit scheme?'
>
> By conflating three elements in a single question, this form of words forces the respondent to take a position on a European redistribution mechanism that would take into account differences in purchasing power between poor and rich countries.
>
> In both these studies, social welfare is presented as a set of benefits for the 'excluded' and the 'poor', rather than as social entitlements accorded to all, such as pension, minimum wage, unemployment benefit, sickness insurance, family support, etc. Nor is the potential existence of European public services taken into account. Given these shortcomings, the large number of non-responses (up to 17 per cent among the working class in Poland) are difficult to interpret, as they reflect the difficulty certain social groups have in expressing an opinion about abstract ideas such as 'social Europe'. Given these biases, caused by the gap between the mindset of those who design them and that of the Europeans they are addressed to, use of data from these European surveys is problematic.

## AN EMBRYONIC EUROPEAN SOCIAL MOVEMENT AND ITS LIMITATIONS

In order for class conflicts to take shape at a European level, social groups would have to establish ways of being represented politically, through signs, symbols and spokespeople. From the 1950s onwards, and still today, the dominant class has been represented in the European arena by federations of employers, lobbies and interest groups. By contrast, trade unions have concentrated most of their efforts in their respective national arena, and the few issues that might have led to Europe-wide campaigns have not taken form in either political or trade union activism at this level.

*European trade unionism in crisis*

Since 1973, the European Trade Union Confederation (ETUC) has represented the main trade unions in member countries in negotiations with European institutions. However, this supranational body remains very remote from activist structures, and its tools are limited owing to the control that governments still maintain over most areas of social welfare.

In the absence of a genuine space of negotiation between representatives of employees and employers at the European level, the ETUC acts more as a locus of training for a trade union elite capable of lobbying European institutions. Since the late 1980s, its activities have consisted primarily of producing expert opinions and lobbying members of the European Parliament to counterbalance the influence of employers' organisations. Having chosen not to play a part in building or coordinating social struggles at a European level, it works primarily in the official spaces accorded it by the European institutions.[40] This choice not to build trade union representation that could campaign directly against the economic and social effects of European treaties is all the more problematic because, as we showed in Chapter 1, the features that members of the working class have in common lie primarily in the sphere of work (deteriorating working conditions, experience of new forms of management, social insecurity, etc.).

Alongside this official trade union structure, there are other forms of representation of employees at supranational level, particularly since the 1994 directive which compels member states to ensure that companies with more than 1,000 employees, operating in two or more EU countries, have works committees.[41] The European Metalworkers' Federation was one of the first to pursue pay claims that extended beyond national boundaries: in 1998

---

40 Richard Hyman, 'Trade Unions and the Politics of European Integration', *Economic and Industrial Democracy* 26: 1, 2005, 9–40.

41 Council of Europe Directive 94/45/CE, of 22 September 1994, on the establishment of a European works committee or a procedure in community-scale undertakings and community-scale groups of undertakings for the purposes of informing and consulting employees.

trade unionists from four countries (Germany, Belgium, Luxembourg and the Netherlands) attempted to set common objectives in relation to pay.[42] But these attempts met with very little success, and trade union organisations remain poorly structured at the European level.

Since the 2008 crisis and its devastating effects in Southern Europe, more and more new activist structures have developed outside traditional trade unions. In Greece, the inability of the General Confederation of Greek Workers (Geniki Synomospondia Ergaton Ellados) to mount an effective opposition to the European troika's diktats led to the emergence of new movements based on local district organisations that brought together people in stable employment with the unemployed, people in precarious jobs and campaigners for self-determination.[43] In Spain, the unions were forced to take a position in relation to the Indignados movement, which succeeded in bringing a number of their demands to the public arena.[44] In Portugal, similarly, new collectives are emerging to represent the demands of workers outside stable employment who are not supported by traditional trade unions.[45] While these campaigns outside the unions have won wide support locally, they do not lend themselves to coordinated initiatives at the European level.

In general, trade unionists have much greater difficulty than political and economic elites in controlling an international space of negotiation, which requires language skills and a capacity to put national reflexes on hold in order to understand the standards

---

42   Anne Dufresne, 'Les enjeux nationaux au cœur de la dimension transnationale du syndicalisme: Le cas du groupe de Doorn (1997–2007)', *Sociologie pratique* 19, 2009, 69–81.

43   Lefteris Kretsos and Markos Vogiatzoglou, 'Lost in the Ocean of Deregulation? The Greek Labour Movement in a Time of Crisis', *Relations industrielles/Industrial Relations* 70: 2, 2015, 218–39.

44   Holm-Detlev Köhler and José Pablo Calleja Jiménez, 'Organizing Heterogeneity: Challenges for the Spanish Trade Unions'. *Transfer: European Review of Labour and Research* 16: 4, 2010, 541–57.

45   Elisio Estanque, Hermes Augusto Costa and José Soeiro, 'The New Global Cycle of Protest and the Portuguese Case', *Journal of Social Science Education* 12: 1, 2013, 31–40.

operating in other countries.[46] Moreover, the economic hierarchies between countries are echoed at trade union level: the Germans, for example, were a driving force in the campaign for a European minimum wage, whereas Italian and Scandinavian trade unionists refused to be involved for fear that they would lose the ability to negotiate at national level.[47] Finally, even when unionists do win some advances within the framework of European social dialogue, these may be neutralised or even cancelled by senior European officials who, under the influence of particular industry groups, refuse to put them on the political agenda of the European Commission.[48]

## European social campaigns that struggle to get beyond national borders

The obstacles to building trade union representation of the working and middle classes at the European level have consequences in terms of the difficulty of organising Europe-wide campaigns.

Following the ratification of the Maastricht treaty, in a context where major industry relocations had taken place and a number of social-democratic governments were in power (France, Germany, United Kingdom), European trade unionists attempted to build transnational campaigns. The announcement, in February 2007, that the Renault plant in Vilvorde (Belgium) was to close, with production relocated to other Renault factories in Europe, was the first trigger. On 7 March, Renault workers in a number of factories in Europe went on strike in solidarity with the Belgian workers, and participated in one of

46   Anne-Catherine Wagner, *Vers une Europe syndicale: Une enquête sur la Confédération européenne des syndicats*, Bellecombe-en-Bauges, Editions du Croquant, 2005.

47   On the issues of a European social policy centred on a European minimum wage, see especially Thorsten Schulten, 'Towards a European Minimum Wage Policy? Fair Wages and Social Europe', *European Journal of Industrial Relations* 14: 4, 2008, 421–39.

48   Julien Louis, 'The Hairdressing Framework Agreement: The European Social Dialogue Struggling with the Field of Eurocracy', paper presented at the conference of the Association française de science politique, 2017, The Field of Eurocracy in Action section.

the first Euro-strikes.[49] On 12 June 1997, 70,000 people marched for jobs through Paris, in a demonstration called by the European Trade Union Confederation, the coordinating body for eighty-two national trade unions in twenty-seven countries, with a total of 60 million members. Two days later, a 'European march against unemployment, poverty and social exclusion' took place in Amsterdam, in a protest organised to coincide with the European summit being held there. Since then, Euro-demonstrations have been organised by alter-globalisation movements in response to every European summit; these movements have also been gathered under the umbrella of the European Social Forums since 2002. These new arenas have gradually found a place in the activist repertoire.[50]

The campaign against the Bolkestein directive was the crowning moment in this sequence of actions, and appears retrospectively as the only trade union initiative that led to the defeat of a European directive.[51] This directive, adopted in January 2004 with the aim of deregulating all service activities in the European Union, first generated hostile reactions in Belgium, a country generally thought to be won over to the European cause. Through the Association for the Taxation of Financial Transactions and Aid to Citizens (ATTAC) network and meetings at the European Social Forum, the campaign quickly spread to France and became incorporated into the campaign against the European constitution. The left in Germany was later in becoming active, and was less strongly mobilised, owing to the split between the social democrats and the radical left, as well as the difficulty of developing a critical discourse on Europe. In these three countries, the success of the campaign was made possible by the alliance between left-wing parties, trade union confederations and the alter-globalisation movement. Despite having

49   Andy Mathers, *Struggling for a Social Europe: Neoliberal Globalization and the Birth of a European Social Movement*, London: Routledge, 2016.

50   Douglas R. Imig and Sidney G. Tarrow, *Contentious Europeans: Protest and Politics in an Emerging Polity*, Lanham, MD: Rowman & Littlefield, 2001.

51   Amandine Crespy, *Qui a peur de Bolkestein? Conflit, résistances et démocratie dans l'Union Européenne*, Paris: Economica, 2012.

officially declared its support of the European constitution, on 19 March 2005 the ETUC organised a demonstration in Brussels that brought together 60,000 people from all over Europe under a single banner: 'More better-quality jobs, defend social Europe, stop Bolkestein'. The alter-globalisation network, already mobilised against the General Agreement on Trade in Services, played a crucial role in the internationalisation of the campaign and the production of an activist expert evaluation, disseminated through the online platform *Stopbolkestein*.[52] The directive was ultimately amended by the European Parliament, which removed the most contentious elements, in one of the few advances won so far by a transnational campaign in Europe. This episode remains symbolic of the split between the working class in the wealthiest European countries and European institutions. But it also marks once more the dominance of activist elites from Northern Europe over those of the South, and still more those of the East.

In these campaigns, the difficulties of generating a set of specific, concrete demands that could unite the working class in all European countries have never really been overcome, except in abstract slogans such as 'Another Europe is possible'. The divisions in the mid-2000s between the alter-globalisation movement, most of whom opposed the European constitution, and the ETUC, which supported it, dealt a serious blow to any possibility of agreement between the various elements of the trade unions and the political left at the European level.

The 2008 financial crisis nevertheless prompted a new cycle of Europe-wide demonstrations against austerity, culminating on 12 November 2012; this day of trade union action organised simultaneously across several countries once again confirmed the regional divisions within Europe. In the South, the one-day general strike was very widely supported among transport and public-service workers, particularly in Spain, where a massive demonstration

---

52 Amandine Crespy, 'A Dialogue of the Deaf? Conflicting Discourses over the EU and Services Liberalization in the WTO', *British Journal of Politics and International Relations* 16: 1, 2014, 168–87.

took place in Madrid. In the East, in Belgium and in France, the day was marked by major demonstrations in a number of cities, and a strike by transport workers in Lithuania. However, in the North and in Germany, the campaign was timid, limited to press releases and statements expressing solidarity with the workers in the South.

This division between a Europe of the South, mobilised against austerity policies, and the countries of the North where strikes are becoming increasingly rare, has not faded. In the 2015 referendum in Greece, the leaders of the ETUC condemned the austerity imposed on the Greek people, but were careful not to challenge the European institutional framework or to take issue with the euro. This resulted in a loss of credibility for them, as it did for the Greek private-sector trade union (GSEE), which is close to PASOK (the Greek socialist party). In the eyes of mobilised workers in the South of Europe, the ETUC is out of step with popular rejection of neoliberal policies, and thus cannot form the leadership of social campaigns. In the field of financial and social rights, as in other sectors where Europe intervenes, the gap between 'advocacy insiders' and 'activist outsiders' has widened.[53]

The absence of a more or less unified social movement at a European level is also due to the difficulties of organising beyond national boundaries: transnational campaigns are costly in terms of time, money and energy. Moreover, the few strikes and demonstrations organised simultaneously in several countries have until now had little impact on the operation and policies of European institutions, and rather resemble a juxtaposition of national interests. The main institutions of the European Union (commission, central bank, etc.) are politically and spatially cut off from European citizens, and leave to national governments the job of implementing the policies enacted by Brussels. Activist citizens, then, find it easier to challenge the national leaders they have elected than the European leaders they do not know. For example, faced with one of the rare Europe-wide demonstrations, which brought together

---

53   Sidney G. Tarrow, *The New Transnational Activism*, Cambridge: Cambridge University Press, 2006.

20,000 trade unionists in Ljubljana in April 2008 to demand a minimum wage in all European countries, Jean-Claude Trichet, then president of the European Central Bank, responded by calling on European countries to exercise wage restraint.

The difficulty that European trade unions have in making European economic governance a political issue is thus partly due to the ability of EU leaders to nationalise social conflicts. The same is true of the directors of major corporations and international companies, who are able to play off subsidiaries against one another in order to neutralise any attempt at resistance.[54]

A further obstacle to formulating demands shared by the whole of the European working class is that their social, educational and cultural world remains highly fragmented and much more disparate than that of the dominant class, as we showed above. Dispersed sites of production, the rise in freelance working, the development of smaller structures and the concomitant decline in major industrial centres all make it less likely that workers will become aware of sharing a common lot. The growth of cities and the rise in private property ownership also play a role in diminishing shared sociability. The symbolic construction of a class is much more likely to arise and endure when the people within it find themselves in close proximity in the social space. The language barrier is another substantial obstacle to the development of a space of collective mobilisation. Building a balance of power involves reflecting on a common language that would allow for dialogue and discussion. The differences in language skills reflect social inequalities that have repercussions for political activism.[55] While English is progressively becoming the European language, language skills remain a powerful marker of discrimination between social groups, despite the fact that among the working class, 'young people' are more comfortable speaking other languages than their elders (see Chapter 3). Better use could be made of new technologies, and the translation tools they offer, until such time as

54 Erne Roland, 'A Supranational Regime That Nationalizes Social Conflict', *Labor History* 56: 3, 2015, 345–68.

55 Jean-Claude Barbier, 'Languages, Political Cultures and Solidarity in Europe', Recode working paper series, 2012, 1–15.

the European Union and national governments invest in a genuine policy of language teaching throughout society. A generalised multi-lingual community is also a possibility, provided that the leaders mediating between groups are able to translate their aspirations to one another politically.

These various obstacles hamper Europe-wide social movements, which until now have remained limited to specific sectors. The railway workers' and lorry drivers' unions, for example, have succeeded in developing shared campaigns, albeit in service of the interests of a male, skilled and relatively mobile sector of the working class.[56] The European campaigns by lorry drivers and rail workers demonstrate concrete attempts to build movements that extend beyond national differences. In April 2018 an initiative by an Austrian cycle couriers' union mobilised delivery staff in Germany, France, the Netherlands, Norway and Italy to coordinate campaigns being waged throughout Europe: a day of action against exploitation, precarious work and union-busting at Deliveroo took place on 13 April 2018. On a different note, dialogue and exchanges between works committee representatives in major corporations also contribute to constructing a European trade union perspective.[57] But these remain isolated examples, and are not enough to establish a repertoire of collective action that could bridge the social and economic divisions between workers in the South and North of Europe.


## CONCLUSION

Although the working class makes up 43 per cent of people at work in Europe, it remains completely absent from EU institutions, and struggles to establish a trade union and political presence at

---

56   Nadia Hilal, *L'eurosyndicalisme par l'action, cheminots et routiers en Europe*, Paris: L'Harmattan, 2007.

57   Elodie Bethoux, 'Vers une représentation européenne des salariés: Les comités d'entreprise européens face aux restructurations', *Sociologie du travail* 51: 4, 2009, 478–98.

European level. The many obstacles to unifying its interests and constituting it as a class mobilised in the European arena have worked greatly to the advantage of radical right-wing parties. These new reactionaries advocate a 'welfare chauvinism' that is all the more popular because the European Union remains synonymous with a tool at the service of liberalism, rather than a body that could provide social benefits to its citizens. In the countries of the East, European laws protecting the basic rights of migrants may even be perceived as an injustice that works in favour of foreigners, to the detriment of integration of Eastern European citizens.[58]

In order to combat the temptation to withdraw behind national frontiers, some intellectuals attempt to use their reputation to help bring together political and trade union movements in European countries. Twenty years ago, Bourdieu's stance on the destructive nature of Europe went roughly alongside the first Europe-wide strikes and trade union campaigns of the 1990s. His article 'For a European Social Movement' called for a return to political campaigning at transnational level. Twenty years later, the promise of these initial mobilisations has not been realised. Given the disdain in which European bodies are held and their inability to relaunch social Europe, some are tempted to propose institutional reforms that would inject greater democracy. The most hotly debated is the proposal for a eurozone parliament with representation proportional to the demographic weight of each country, which would determine budgetary policy, the revival of the European economy and the regulation of national debts.[59] While this solution may be intellectually appealing, it nevertheless still entrusts the destiny of the European Union to the goodwill of European elites (lawyers, senior officials, etc.), without resolving the deficit of representation and participation of the working class.

58  Ivan Krastev, *After Europe*, Philadelphia: University of Pennsylvania Press, 2017.

59  Sophie Hennette, Thomas Piketty, Guillaume Sacriste and Antoine Vauchez, *How to Democratize Europe*, Cambridge, MA: Harvard University Press, 2019.

It is therefore doubtful that it would be sufficient to revive the project of social Europe, particularly if all other treaties remain the same. The mobilisation of social classes within the European space is a much longer and more chaotic process than the movement whereby European leaders have imposed a common economic policy. Two conditions are necessary for the emergence of a European social movement: the existence of transnational trade union structures and the development of lasting socialisation links between workers from different countries.[60] Some particularly brutal measures, such as those taken against countries of the South following the 2008 crisis, may speed up the awakening of the working class to awareness of their shared lot. But, in a space that is home to twenty-eight nationalities and millions of workers speaking different languages, the work of unification remains to be done. It should be the priority of trade union organisations, NGOs and political parties who claim to be on the left. The success of the campaign against the Bolkestein directive shows that when these different activist movements come together they can play a decisive role in the construction of a European social movement. The need to develop a balance of power favourable to working and middle classes in Europe is more pressing than ever. It is the only way that genuine popular sovereignty can assert itself in the face of the dominance of capital in Europe.

60   Katarzyna Gajewska, 'The Emergence of a European Labour Protest Movement?', *European Journal of Industrial Relations* 14: 1, 2008, 104–21.

# Conclusion

The choice made in this book to use social groups to describe Europe is not a usual one: it makes visible inequalities that the class-blind approach of European leaders conceals. By studying inequalities among social groups, our results go beyond the strict framework of employment; they reflect economic, cultural and political divisions and allow us to glimpse oppositions between social groups on a European scale. Many other determinants, such as generational belonging, minority status or territorial location, are more visible in the public space, with the result that the working class remains a political issue only through the term 'populism' used as a spectre. In most European countries, social-democratic parties have deliberately abandoned the defence of those workers most exposed to neoliberal logic and even implemented reforms that weaken and marginalise them.

In a context of financialisation of the economy and the triumph of free trade, relations between social classes are largely determined at the European level and no longer simply within a national framework. The circulation of economic capital, of cultural and symbolic goods, cuts across national borders, as likewise does the restructuring of firms. The migration of workers, students and tourists means that millions of European citizens have direct and concrete experience of class relations on a continental scale. These confrontations are not only between workers of the richer Europe and those in the East and South, as the result of relocation or outsourced work. European capitalism also places bosses and managers in competition with each other, driven to reorganise working conditions in factories established in countries where labour is cheaper. As for the European Union's policy, this contributes significantly to reinforcing social inequalities throughout the continent and is proving incapable of meeting environmental challenges that ever more clearly contradict the interests of multinational firms. Until now, sensitivity to the climate emergency has been most prevalent in Western and Northern countries, but it could bring together alliances that go beyond national particularisms, particularly among the younger generations.

Regardless of its flaunted 'independence', the European Central Bank has steadily established itself as the best guarantee against the vagaries of universal suffrage in the twenty-seven member states. The constraint it places on national budgets targets both public services and the viability of social protection systems and rights at work, in both cases hitting the middle and working classes. The advantage of considering social classes on the continent as a whole is that it highlights the characteristics shared by their members regardless of their country of residence. For the working class, there is greater exposure to unemployment and precariousness than in any other social group, more arduous working conditions, a position of economic subordination and relative exclusion from cultural practices such as the mastery of foreign languages or new technologies. Among the dominant classes, despite the income disparities that separate the super-executives in finance from other highly qualified professions, there are many elements of convergence: their members enjoy greater autonomy in the field of work, and can reconcile professional life, family life and leisure more readily than other workers. More fundamentally, they combine economic, cultural, linguistic and political resources, and a majority of them support the project of European integration, unlike the working class. Though representations of society in terms of classes have tended to decline, inequalities between social groups have actually deepened since the 1980s, with cumulative effects for young people, women and minorities.

The 'European question' has thus become in recent years a central issue in political struggles, not only in the various referendums on the future of the European Union, but also in national elections. The class conflicts expressed in these represent a division between a large part of the working class and often the middle class (small employers, lower-grade officials) on the one hand, and the dominant class on the other. For all that, this expression of a class struggle on the European scale remains confined within the national electoral framework. It is also denied by commentators and politicians who condemn, from a moral point of view, votes that reject EU policy, interpreting them as 'reactionary' or 'populist' temptations, without ever linking them to the neoliberal policy that is at the root of these electoral sanctions. Indeed, the social demands made by the Euro-demonstrations, Euro-strikes and European social forums of the late 1990s and early 2000s were met with intransigence by European leaders. Moreover, far from arising from stable identities, the class divisions described in this book also correspond to different forms of politicisation. Thus the European working class is the social group that has paid the heaviest price for the 2008 crisis, while its mobilisations and trade union commitment has remained very disparate. Most of the resistance actually came from young graduates with an uncertain professional future and from the middle class in the public sector, faced with austerity policies and deteriorating working conditions. These heterogeneous reactions are very likely an additional sign of the growing difficulty that the victims of the crisis have in recognising themselves in terms of class identities and reappropriating these as central to mobilisation.

Finally, the circulation of capital on a European scale fuels or even amplifies divergences between the social structures of the different countries: the working class appears to be divided between those in the North of the continent, who possess a certain economic affluence as measured by the facilities they enjoy and a still-rising level of qualification, and those in the South and East, who remain confined to situations of poverty and extreme precariousness. In a highly competitive economy in which capital is readily mobile, this gap leads to competition and social dumping between these two fractions of the European working class. A convergence of demands among groups at the bottom of the social space is all the less likely, given that social protection systems remain highly differentiated between these two parts of Europe: thanks to their national states, the working class in the North benefits from social safety nets that are disproportionate to what exists in the East and the South. At the other end of the European social space, the dominant class of the Northern countries is interconnected, and hardly threatened by competition from that of the Southern and Eastern countries. Its horizon seems clear and the European framework that is being constructed even provides it with a series of resources for establishing domination in each national space.

Heterogeneity of social structures and the erasure of class adherence contribute to perpetuating a paradoxical situation: although in a minority, the members of the middle and dominant classes who support the European Union project manage to remain in the political majority.[1] In the absence of a political alternative, the radical and far right can thus thrive on hostility to the neoliberalism imposed by the European shackles, both in the former Eastern Bloc countries and in Austria, France, the United Kingdom, the Netherlands and Italy. This movement is partly the result of the lack of an economic perspective for the working and middle classes affected by the crisis. The feat of the ultra-conservatives is to have succeeded in transforming social discontent into national withdrawal, in a scenario that has parallels with that of the interwar period. The particularity of the current period is that the dominant class continues to believe in and defend the European project, despite the explosive social situations it has generated in Greece, Portugal, Spain and even the United Kingdom.

While attempts to reform the European Union in a more 'social' direction have failed,[2] an increasing number of parties of the radical left are considering a possible exit from the European Union or at least the eurozone: La France Insoumise, the Portuguese Left Bloc, Podemos in Spain, Die Linke in Germany, etc. For many of them, defending the protective framework of the national state can be a short-term response to social dumping and the dismantling of the public sector. If for many years a radical questioning of the EU seemed unthinkable on the left, it now emerges as a plausible hypothesis. Other movements also rooted in the left are calling

---

1   Bruno Amable and Stefano Palombarini, 'The *bloc bourgeois* in France and Italy', in Hideko Magara (ed.), *Economic Crises and Policy Regimes*, Cheltenham: Edward Elgar Publishing, 2014, 177–216.

2   Amandine Crespy and Georg Menz (eds), *Social Policy and the Eurocrisis: Quo Vadis Social Europe*, Basingstoke: Palgrave Macmillan, 2015.

for a reform of institutions that could guarantee genuine representative democracy and transparency of deliberations. Among the solutions most discussed is the demand for a eurozone parliament with deliberative power, composed of elected representatives fairly representing all member countries.[3]

This debate has the advantage of reminding the European institutions of their social and democratic obligations, given that they now seem discredited representatives of social interests that are opposed to those of the greatest number. Undoubtedly, the question of continued membership of the European Union and the eurozone has the merit of placing economic issues at the heart of class conflicts at the European level.

However, these strategic positions towards the European Union are currently receiving relatively little attention from the European population. The question of the repeal of the treaties or the necessary institutional reforms remains for the majority of Europeans still very abstract, arousing indifference rather than rejection or support. To build a balance of power at the European level that is favourable to the working and middle classes beyond national differences will require articulating demands that meet the immediate concerns of these populations and can be immediately transposed to the European scale, the terrain on which capitalist firms operate. For example, we can imagine social convergence criteria that replace those of the Stability and Growth Pact adopted following the Maastricht agreements. This could be the setting of a 3 per cent unemployment target, above which countries would be sanctioned by fines used to support workers who have been laid off. It could also be a maximum rate of precariousness, beyond which governments would be forced to compensate those who suffer this form of exploitation. By initiating a project that highlights the need for a European labour law, social protection and public services, and drawing on the opportunities offered by digital technologies, trade unions and voluntary organisations could propose systems of solidarity and protection favourable

---

3 Sophie Hennette, Thomas Piketty, Guillaume Sacriste and Antoine Vauchez, *How to Democratize Europe*, Cambridge, MA: Harvard University Press, 2019.

to the most precarious occupational groups, such as Uber drivers or Deliveroo workers. As this book has shown, experience of hardship and suffering at work is the common ground between members of the working and middle classes; to mobilise groups that have succumbed to resignation, it seems necessary to make the transformation of work a central political issue, especially since it is now linked to ecological questions. On the basis of a reorganisation of work to be less hierarchical and more respectful of health and the environment, we can also imagine alliances between the working class, intellectuals, engineers and technicians. More fundamentally, it is time for left-wing parties, militant trade unions and voluntary organisations to name and make visible the class inequalities that are eating away at European solidarity. In the absence of representation by spokespersons who embody their concerns and defend their interests in Brussels, sections of the working class risk preferring the solution of national withdrawal, which is so far the only one to offer them meagre protection. It is by rebuilding at European level what neoliberal policies have destroyed at the national level that we can hope to construct a balance of power favourable to populations suffering the damage caused by neoliberalism.

# Secondary Use of Four European Surveys

There are two types of statistical source available at the European level. First, there are data similar to opinion polls, which are based on limited samples and often gathered by quota sampling. Second, there are studies carried out by the national statistical bodies based on much larger samples and a random sampling method that allows non-response bias to be better taken into account. In composing our portrait of social class in Europe, we drew primarily on this second type of source. We based our analysis on combined use of three European studies conducted under the aegis of Eurostat (the European Union Statistical Office): the Labour Force Survey (LFS, 2011 and 2014 editions), the European Union Statistics on Income and Living Conditions (EU-SILC, 2006 and 2014 editions) and the Adult Education Survey (AES, 2011 edition). We also drew on the European Working Conditions Survey (EWCS 2015), designed by researchers and financed by Eurofound, the European Foundation for the Improvement of Living and Working Conditions.

The Labour Force Survey (LFS) is compiled by aggregating European national surveys of the labour market. It generates the main indicators of the labour market, such as rate of unemployment and employment. The number of variables standardised for all European countries (known as 'core variables') is limited, but they do document part-time working, temporary contracts, unsocial working hours, activity sector, and level of urbanisation of Europeans. It is a large-scale Europe-wide survey of 1.5 million individuals, selected every three months (i.e. 4.4 million for the year 2014) in proportions ranging from 0.2 per cent to 3.3 per cent, depending on the country. Data relate to all of the twenty-seven EU member states, as well as Croatia (which joined the EU in 2013), Iceland, Norway, Switzerland, the Republic of Macedonia and Turkey.

The European Union Statistics on Income and Living Conditions Survey (EU-SILC) is a longitudinal study that aims to measure various forms of poverty and exclusion. Households are asked about their income, housing, standard of living, level of education, health and work. It has existed in this format since 2003, and covers 130,000 households and 273,000 individuals aged sixteen or over. The permanent core section focuses on questions of poverty and exclusion. The variable modules that supplement this each year are also concerned with these issues. We used the 2006 'social-participation' module, which related to cultural leisure pursuits and involvement in community groups and trade unions.

The Adult Education Survey (AES) surveys households every five years, and focuses specifically on life-long learning. Individuals aged between twenty-five and sixty-four are asked about their participation in education and training. We used the 2011 study, conducted in thirty countries with 225,000 individuals, particularly the questions relating to cultural practices, skills in new information and communication technologies (NICT), the Internet and foreign languages.

Access to the microdata in these first three studies was granted under an agreement with Eurostat. The results and conclusions drawn from our use of them are entirely those of the authors of this book and in no way those of Eurostat.

The European Working Conditions Survey (EWCS) is conducted every five years by the Dublin-based European Foundation for the Improvement of Living and Working Conditions (Eurofound). It aims to supply comparable and reliable data for all European countries, to analyse the relationships between different aspects of working conditions, and to identify the groups exposed to risk, but also those whose conditions are improving. The data used in the present study come from the sixth edition of the survey, conducted in thirty-five countries in 2015.

More than 43,000 individuals aged fifteen and over, employed and living in the country surveyed, were interviewed. The face-to-face interviews took place in the respondents' homes. In one place we have also used data from the fifth version of this survey (2010), on the question of financial consequences of an error at work, which no longer appeared in the 2015 questionnaire.

In our use of these four European surveys, we focused on people in work, aged from twenty-five to sixty-five, living in the European Union (EU 27, excluding Malta). We restricted our study to those in work because of the poor quality of coding of last job occupied for unemployed people in most European countries.

There were some geographical variations in survey population in our analyses, for a number of reasons:

**Quality of data related to profession**: Malta (all surveys) and Slovenia (EU-SILC 2014) only code the socio-economic position of respondents at the aggregated level of the 2008 International Standard Classification of Occupations (see Appendix 2 below), meaning that no ESEG classification can be compiled for these countries. This is also the case for Bulgaria and Romania for the social-participation module (EU-SILC 2006). We therefore excluded these countries from these surveys or modules.

**Quality of data related to leisure**: in the 2006 EU-SILC survey, we excluded countries with a high non-response level (Netherlands and Ireland) and countries where the questionnaire was translated in a very different way from others (Austria and Finland).

**Non-response of some countries to particular questions**: the AES includes a number of non-compulsory modules. On reading practices, Denmark, Belgium, the United Kingdom, France, the Netherlands and Sweden gave no response. On Internet skills, Denmark, the Netherlands and the United Kingdom gave no response. On NITC skills, only the United Kingdom failed to respond.

# Construction of Social Classes at European Level Using the ESEG Classification

This book uses the ESEG (European Socio-economic Groups) classification, produced as a result of a study coordinated by INSEE at the request of Eurostat. It was drawn up with the collaboration of statisticians and researchers from France, Hungary, Italy and the Czech Republic, on the basis of earlier studies conducted from the 1990s onwards. The aim of this new tool is to better measure social processes and their development in Europe, using standardised categories of social stratification.

This European socio-economic classification is based on the most recent version of the International Standard Classification of Occupations (ISCO-08). The 2008 ISCO takes level of education into account more than the previous version (ISCO-88) did, and incorporates supervisory duties (for example, some manual workers with supervisory duties have been reclassified as 'intermediate professionals'). The ESEG classification is especially useful because it incorporates the employment status of those surveyed (employed or self-employed). It opens up new possibilities for identifying and evaluating social inequalities and comparing them at the European level.

However, the way the different socio-economic groups are constructed in each country varies substantially, making this classification a very imperfect tool. While overall the relative positions of socio-economic groups are similar throughout Europe, there are variations for some of them. Groups such as drivers (ESEG 65) and teachers (ESEG 25) are relatively clearly identified in each European country, but some distinctions are less clear in some countries. This is the case, for example, with the division between 'nurses and associate health professionals' (ESEG 32) and 'doctors and healthcare professionals' (ESEG 22), which is based on a distinction between midwives and nurses depending on whether they are coded as 'associate professionals' (group 3) or 'professionals' (group 2), which appears to vary from country to country in ISCO-08. These differences in coding relate partly to the flexibility Eurostat allows when certain surveys are set up. The complete ESEG classification comprises nine main groups and forty-two subgroups. For people in work, the aggregated level comprises seven groups, while what is known as the detailed level is made up of thirty subgroups (see Appendix 3 below).

In order to analyse social inequality at the European level, we combined various features of the thirty socio-economic groups in the classification. Our multidimensional approach to inequality in Europe was based on observation of different aspects of social hierarchies, cross-referencing possession of various kinds of capital (financial, cultural) with working environment (position, sector and working conditions). We used a number of indicators for this purpose. Equivalised disposable household income (by European quartile) and level of education (higher or further education, secondary, or lower than secondary) are fairly widely accepted indicators of financial and cultural capital in studies of social stratification. Among employees, supervisory duties mark an asymmetric position in the workplace that relates to a social hierarchy. Constructing a variable that distinguishes between employees in public occupations (or the public sector), employees in private sectors, and the self-employed offers a better way of assessing different relations to the state. We used two indicators related to working hours (frequent working in free time, and regularity of working hours each week) in order to take into account both the flexibility and the time commitment required by some jobs, especially for the self-employed, and the balance between private and work life. Finally, the use of body position (seated or standing) marks the distinction between indoor work activities (in an office, moving little) and outdoor work (farming, construction and even industry), where workers move about more.

Principal component analysis (Graph 3) outlines a European social space where, on the vertical axis, subjects belonging to the wealthiest households in Europe (members of households in the fourth European income quartile), who have higher education and supervise others in their workplace, sit at the top. At the bottom of the vertical axis are subjects belonging to the poorest households in Europe (members of households in the first European income quartile), whose qualifications are below high-school leaving certificate and who work standing up. The horizontal axis reveals another opposition with, on the left, employed individuals who have regular working hours and tend to be members of households in the third European income quartile, and, on the right, freelance (self-employed) individuals who state that they very often work during their free time. Thus we have a number of significant indices for identifying the key subgroups at the top, middle and bottom of the European social space.

At the top are the subgroups ESEG 13 (senior managers), ESEG 21 (engineers and specialists in science, engineering and information technology (IT)), ESEG 22 (doctors and healthcare specialists), ESEG 23 (administration, finance and business managers) and ESEG 24 (lawyers, judges, journalists, artists). At the bottom is the cluster of ESEG 53 (nursing assistants, childcare workers, home-care assistants), ESEG 61 (skilled construction workers), ESEG 62 (skilled craft or food and drink industry workers), Eseg 63 (workers in the metalwork and electronics industries), ESEG 64 (machine operators), ESEG 65 (drivers), ESEG 71 (retail and service assistants), ESEG 72 (manual labourers), ESEG 73 (cleaners) and ESEG 74 (farm employees) – the employee groups that make up the bulk of the working class in Europe. ESEG 41 (farmers) and ESEG 43 (craftsmen) sit close to these groups on the vertical axis, but at the opposite end of the horizontal axis. Between these two extremes an intermediate zone ranges from ESEG 25 (teachers) to ESEG 12 (self-employed hotel and restaurant owners). Two main sub-clusters of occupations can be distinguished here. One is closer to the least qualified and poorest ESEG subgroups: this consists of ESEG 54 (police officers, armed service personnel and security agents), Eseg 52 (receptionists and customer service clerks) and ESEG 51 (office workers). The cluster above them on

*Graph 3. A Representation of the European Social Space,
Based on a Number of Surveys. Factorial Plan of PCA*

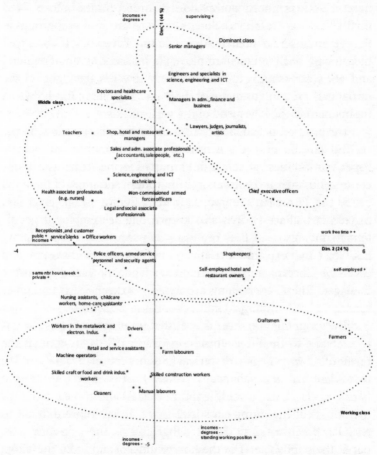

*Note*: People in work aged twenty-five to sixty-five, EU 27 (excluding
Malta for LFS 2014; excluding Malta and Slovenia for EU-SILC 2014;
excluding Malta for EWCS 2015). The full titles of the ESEG groups are
given in Appendix 3, p. 195.
*Sources*: LFS 2014; EU-SILC 2014; EWCS 2015.

the vertical axis consists of ESEG 31 (science, engineering and ICT technicians), ESEG 32 (health associate professionals, e.g. nurses), ESEG 33 (sales and administration associate professionals (accountants)), ESEG 34 (legal and social associate profession-nals), ESEG 35 (non-commissioned armed forces officers) and finally ESEG 25 (teachers), those closest to the ESEG subgroups at the top. In this intermediate zone, two subgroups of self-employed individuals, ESEG 12 (self-employed hotel and restaurant owners) and ESEG 42 (shopkeepers) sit clearly towards the right on the horizontal axis, in parallel with ESEG 41 (farmers) and ESEG 43 (craftsmen) at the lower end of the vertical axis.

The position of ESEG 11 (chief executive officer) is low on the vertical axis, a fact that is explained primarily by the fact that the supervisory-duties variable is not reported for self-employed work-ers. Second, their income varies more widely, and more of them fall below the European median than in ESEG 14 (shop, hotel and restaurant managers). It is also known that self-employed people tend to underestimate their professional income more than employ-ees, which may explain the relatively lower income of ESEG 11 (chief executive officer) compared to ESEG 14 (shop, hotel and restaurant managers. These observations prompted us to keep ESEG 11 (higher managerial self-employed) in the dominant-class group.

The grouping into three classes that we propose in this book is represented by the three ellipses on Graph 3. This grouping is the result of a two-pronged, empirical and theoretical, evaluation. We first identified the subgroups typically situated at the bottom (working class), in the middle (middle class) and at the top (domi-nant class) of the European social space. It was more difficult to allocate the remaining ESEG subgroups – the self-employed, particularly ESEG 11 (chief executive officer) and ESEG 14 (shop, hotel and restaurant managers) to one social class rather than another purely on the basis of the results of this PCA. This division into three social classes follows social science convention. It remains schematic and is primarily a working tool, influenced both by the tenuousness of the internal distinctions within each ESEG socio-economic group and by variations in the coding of professions in different countries, noted above.

# ESEG Classification (Detailed Level) and Social Class

Table 15. *European Socio-economic Groups*

ESEG 2

| | | |
|---|---|---|
| 11 | Chief executive officers | 1% |
| 13 | Senior managers | 3.5% |
| 21 | Engineers and specialists in science, engineering and information technology | 5% |
| 22 | Doctors and healthcare specialists | 3% |
| 23 | Managers in administration, finance and business | 4% |
| 24 | Lawyers, judges, journalists, artists | 2.5% |
| | **Total European dominant class** | **19%** |
| 12 | Self-employed hotel and restaurant owners | 1% |
| 14 | Shop, hotel and restaurant managers | 1% |
| 25 | Teachers | 5% |
| 31 | Science, engineering and ICT technicians | 4% |
| 32 | Health associate professionals (e.g. nurses) | 2.5% |
| 33 | Sales and administration associate professionals (accountants, salespeople, etc.) | 6% |
| 34 | Legal and social associate professionnals | 1% |
| 35 | Non-commissioned armed forces officers | 0.5% |
| 42 | Shopkeepers | 5% |
| 51 | Office workers | 7% |
| 52 | Receptionists and customer service clerks | 1% |

| 54 | Police officers, armed service personnel and security agents | 1% |
|---|---|---|
| | **Total European middle class** | **38%** |
| 41 | Farmers | 3% |
| 43 | Craftsmen | 3.5% |
| 53 | Nursing assistants, childcare workers, home-care assistants | 3% |
| 61 | Skilled construction workers | 2.5% |
| 62 | Skilled craft or food and drink industry workers | 1.5% |
| 63 | Workers in the metalwork and electronics industries | 5% |
| 64 | Machine operators | 3% |
| 65 | Drivers | 4% |
| 71 | Retail and service assistants | 8% |
| 72 | Manual labourers | 4.5% |
| 73 | Cleaners | 4% |
| 74 | Farm labourers | 1% |
| | **Total European working class** | **43%** |

Note: People in work aged twenty-five to sixty-five. LFS 2014, EU 27 (excluding Malta)

# Constructing a European
# Social Class Space

Grouping occupations into three main social classes provides a means of comparing social position in the twenty-six countries under consideration. The resulting seventy-eight 'social class countries' (twenty-six countries times three social classes) served as the framework for Chapter 5.

We combined principal component analysis (PCA) of the financial and educational resources, employment status and sector and conditions of employment of these social class countries with an ascending hierarchical classification (AHC) in order to obtain a picture of the relative positions of social classes in the European space. This description compares, on the one hand, financial and cultural resources, on the basis of equivalised disposable household income (by European quartile), and, on the other, the morphologies of jobs in different social classes in different countries, based on supervisory duties, employment status (employed or self-employed), work sector (public or private) and part-time working. We had two reasons for using this latter indicator: to take into account the gendered composition of the social class countries, and to incorporate the intra-national effects of some countries' employment policies.

The PCA/AHC draws a map of social classes in Europe, and allow us to identify six groups of social class countries (Graph 4):

**Group 1**, at the top of the social hierarchy, comprises the dominant classes in the countries of the North and West of Europe. The proportions of individuals figuring among the wealthiest Europeans (fourth quartile of disposable household income), of individuals with supervisory duties and of individuals with higher education qualifications are significantly higher than in all other groups.

**Group 2** comprises the dominant classes in the countries of the East and some of those in the South (Portugal, Greece), and is also characterised by significant numbers of individuals with supervisory duties and higher education qualifications. However, their income is not statistically distinct from that of other groups.

**Group 3** comprises the middle classes in the countries of the North and West of Europe, and the dominant classes in the Netherlands. This group represents the wealthiest middle class in Europe (third and fourth income quartiles), among whom employees in the public and quasi-public sector and part-time employees are over-represented.

**Group 4** comprises the middle class in the countries of the East and some countries of the South (Portugal, Greece). Here again, public-sector employees are over-represented compared to the other groups, but these are among the least wealthy middle classes in Europe (second and first quartiles).

**Group 5** comprises the working class of the countries of the North and West of Europe. It includes a high proportion of individuals with qualifications below high-school leaving certificate, individuals in part-time work, and commercial-sector employees.

**Group 6** comprises the working class in the countries of the East and some countries of the South (Portugal, Greece). Like Group 5, it includes many employees in the commercial sector; in this group the poorest Europeans are over-represented, but the level of education is considerably higher than among the working class of the North and West.

*Graph 4. A Typology of the Different Social Classes in Europe, Based on the Results of Several Surveys*

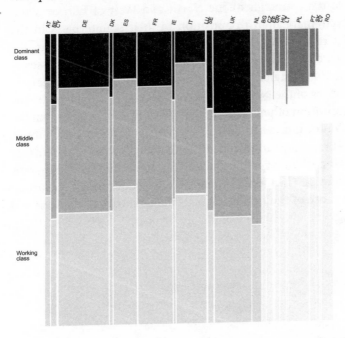

Notes: People in work aged between twenty-five and sixty-five. EU 27 (excluding Malta for LFS 2014; excluding Malta and Slovenia for EU-SILC 2014). AT = Austria, BE = Belgium, CY = Cyprus, DE = Germany, DK = Denmark, ES = Spain, FR = France, IE = Ireland, IT = Italy, LU = Luxembourg, SE = Sweden, UK = United Kingdom, NL = Netherlands, BG = Bulgaria, CZ = Czech Republic, EE = Estonia, GR = Greece, HU = Hungary, LT = Lithuania, PL = Poland, PT = Portugal, SK = Slovakia, LV = Latvia, RO = Romania. Note: The ascending hierarchical classification presented here is based on PCA of the seventy-two social class countries (first five axes). The three social classes of Finland are placed individually, for the purposes of illustration, in the PCA of the social class countries, in view of the significant proportion of non-responses in the social position variable (ISCO-08) in LFS 2014. The boxes represent social class (row) per country (column). Their size is proportional to their relative weight among people in work in Europe.
*Sources*: LFS 2014; EU-SILC 2014.

Thus in terms of their financial and cultural resources and conditions of employment, the working, middle and dominant classes of the countries of the North and West of Europe stand almost systematically in opposition to their counterparts in the countries of the East, Portugal and Greece. With respect to the variables we took into consideration, only the dominant classes of the Netherlands stand out, being classed with the middle class of the countries of the North and West. This can be explained by the large proportion of people in part-time work, and the fact that the proportion of individuals with supervisory duties is substantially lower than in other countries. Among the countries of the former Soviet Bloc, the dominant classes in Latvia and Romania show characteristics (including financial and educational resources) close to those of the middle class in the countries of the East and South.

# Index